Reimagining Police

Privatizing Law and Order

Lisa Stolzenberg & Stewart J. D'Alessio

Use of AI

Publishing.ai was used as part of the manuscript development workflow for organizational and editorial support. The authors revised, reviewed and finalized the manuscript and assume full responsibility for its content.

Table of Content

Introduction

In an era where public trust in law enforcement is at a historic low, can we afford to continue with the status quo? The challenges facing our police forces are not new, but they have reached a tipping point. Overburdened, underfunded, and increasingly scrutinized, public policing is struggling to meet the demands of 21st-century society. But what if there was another way? What if the solution to our policing crisis lies not in reform but reimagining?

Enter private policing. It's a concept that may seem foreign, even uncomfortable, to many. After all, the idea of outsourcing such a fundamental public service to private entities raises legitimate concerns about accountability, equity, and the very nature of our social contract. However, the reality is that private policing is already here, and it's growing. From gated communities to corporate campuses, from shopping malls to universities, private security personnel are increasingly assuming roles traditionally reserved for public police.

However, this book is not a blind endorsement of privatization. Rather, it is an invitation to a much-needed conversation. As college students, educators, and policymakers, you are the future leaders who will shape the direction of law enforcement. Therefore, you deserve a comprehensive understanding of the forces driving the expansion of private policing, the potential benefits and risks it presents, and the critical policy questions it raises.

Through rigorous analysis, case studies from around the globe, and practical policy recommendations, *Reimagining Police: Privatizing Law and Order* will take you on a journey through the past, present, and potential future of private policing. We'll trace its historical roots, examine its current manifestations, and explore its implications on issues ranging from civil liberties to social equity.

In this sense, this book is more than just an academic exercise. As authors, our passion for this topic is deeply personal. Having witnessed firsthand the struggles of public police to meet the needs of communities, we believe we owe it to ourselves and future generations to consider all options for improving public safety. Our goal is not to persuade you of a particular viewpoint but to equip you with the knowledge and tools to engage in this critical dialogue.

Whether you're a criminal justice student grappling with the future of your profession, a public policy major seeking innovative solutions to societal challenges, or a concerned citizen trying to make sense of a changing world, this book is for you. By the end of it, you may not have all the answers, but you will have the right questions. Hence, you will be prepared to participate in one of the most consequential debates of our time: How do we ensure safety, justice, and equity in a world where the lines between public and private are increasingly blurred?

So, let's embark on this journey together. Let's challenge our assumptions, confront uncomfortable realities, and imagine possibilities. The future of policing is not predetermined; it will be shaped by the choices we make and the conversations we have. This book is my invitation to you to be part of that conversation. Are you ready?

Chapter 1:

The Evolution of Private Policing

The concept of private policing may seem like a modern development, but its roots stretch back thousands of years. To understand where we are today, we need to consider the long, winding road that led us here. Picture a bustling Roman street in the first century, where the Vigiles, an ancient corps of watchmen and firefighters, kept a vigilant eye on the city. They were among the earliest forms of organized protection, serving the community by patrolling the streets to prevent fires and maintain order. These early efforts in Rome laid the groundwork for what would eventually evolve into the private security we know today.

From Watchmen to Security Firms: A Historical Overview

In ancient Rome, the Vigiles patrolled the streets not just as enforcers of law but as protectors against the ever-present threat of fire, a constant menace in the densely packed city. These watchmen were part of a system that emphasized community safety, blending public duty with the practical needs of urban life. Fast forward to the medieval era, and you'd find Night Watchmen pacing the cobblestone streets of European towns, their lanterns casting flickering shadows as they called out the hours. These individuals were often local townsfolk, tasked with protecting their neighbors from thieves and fires during the vulnerable nighttime hours. The shift from Roman Vigiles to medieval Night Watchmen illustrates the enduring need for organized security adapted to fit the societal context of the time.

As societies continued to evolve, so too did the structures of protection. Guild protection services emerged as skilled tradespeople banded together to safeguard their interests. Members of these guilds pooled resources to hire guards, establishing an early form of collective security. This ensured their goods and markets were protected, reflecting a growing recognition of the economic benefits of organized security.

By the time the industrial revolution rolled around, society had changed dramatically. Cities swelled with new inhabitants, and with them came new challenges. Subsequently, urban crime surged as economic disparity grew, placing unprecedented pressure on existing public policing systems. It was in this climate that the Bow Street Runners came into being in the 18th century, serving as one of the first professional police forces in London. Their formation marked a pivotal shift from informal groups to structured policing entities, laying the groundwork for what would become modern private security.

Later, the 19th and 20th centuries saw the birth of private security firms, a direct response to the limitations of public law enforcement. Allan Pinkerton, with his Pinkerton National Detective Agency, became a pioneering figure in this transformation. Established in 1850, Pinkerton's agency specialized in railway theft cases, protecting trains and cargo across the burgeoning American landscape. This agency gained fame for solving high-profile crimes, like the $700,000 Adams Express Co. theft in 1866. Pinkerton's work even included thwarting an assassination plot against President-Elect Abraham Lincoln, showcasing the agency's pivotal role in national security matters. The legacy of the Pinkerton Agency set the stage for future private security firms, emphasizing the potential for these organizations to fill gaps left by public policing.

Furthermore, the emergence of firms like the Wackenhut Corporation further solidified the role of private security in the 20th century. Founded in 1954, Wackenhut expanded rapidly, offering a range of services from guarding nuclear facilities to providing corporate security. This expansion was driven by a combination of economic and social factors. Industrialization and urbanization increased the demand for asset protection, as businesses and individuals sought to safeguard their interests in an increasingly interconnected world. The rise of the urban middle class contributed to this phenomenon, as economic growth fueled greater consumption and, subsequently, a heightened need for security services.

Throughout history, private policing has been shaped by the society it serves. Economic shifts, technological advancements, and social transformations have each played a role in its evolution. From the watchful eyes of the Vigiles to the strategic operations of modern security firms, the story of private policing is one of adaptation and innovation. As we continue to explore this complex landscape, you'll see how these historical roots inform today's debates on the role of private security in our communities.

The Rise of Private Security: Key Milestones

In the tapestry of modern security, certain threads stand out as pivotal moments that shaped the landscape of private policing. One such thread was the introduction of alarm systems in the late 19th and early 20th centuries. These early systems, though rudimentary by today's standards, marked a significant technological leap. They offered businesses and homeowners a sense of security previously unattainable by human presence alone.

The advent of these systems was not just about installing devices; it was a step toward integrating technology into security strategies, foreshadowing the digital revolutions that would redefine security in the decades to come. As alarm systems became more sophisticated, they laid the groundwork for the next phase of private security: the establishment of global security firms. These companies expanded their reach beyond local markets, setting up operations in multiple countries and offering a wide range of services, from personal protection to large-scale event security. This globalization of security services reflected the interconnectedness of the modern world and the universal need for safety and protection.

Historical Events

Historical events have always been catalysts for change, and the field of private security is no exception. During World War II, the demand for security services surged, driven by the need to protect critical infrastructure and sensitive information. In addition, the war effort accelerated technological advancements, leading to innovations in communications and surveillance that would later be adapted for civilian use.

In the aftermath of 9/11, the landscape of private security underwent another transformation. The attacks highlighted significant gaps in public safety, prompting a dramatic increase in the demand for private security services. Subsequently, companies invested heavily in security infrastructure, integrating advanced technologies like biometric systems and data analytics to enhance their capabilities. This era also witnessed the rise of comprehensive security solutions, combining physical and digital safeguards to address the complex threats of the modern age.

Legislation

Legislation has played a crucial role in defining and refining the parameters within which private security operates. The Private Security Industry Act 2001 in the UK stands as a landmark in the regulation of the industry. It established the Security Industry Authority (SIA), which set standards for licensing and conduct, ensuring that private security personnel met rigorous criteria before being allowed to operate. This act not only professionalized the industry but also provided a framework for accountability, addressing public concerns about the oversight of private security firms.

In the United States, licensing and regulatory frameworks have similarly evolved, varying by state but generally emphasizing the need for background checks, training, and adherence to ethical guidelines. These legislative measures reflect a growing recognition of the importance of private security in maintaining public safety and order.

Major Events

The role of private security in major public events cannot be overstated. Take, for example, the Olympic Games. These global spectacles require meticulous planning and execution to ensure the safety of thousands of athletes and spectators. Therefore, private security firms are often called upon to supplement public efforts, providing specialized expertise and resources. Their involvement is not limited to physical security; it extends to cybersecurity, crowd management, and emergency response planning.

Corporate events, too, have become arenas where private security is indispensable. High-profile gatherings, such as shareholder meetings and product launches, attract significant attention and require comprehensive security measures. In this setting, firms provide not only the manpower to secure these events but also the technological tools to monitor and respond to potential threats in real-time.

Private security's evolution is a testament to its adaptability and innovation in the face of changing societal needs. As we navigate an increasingly complex world, these milestones serve as reminders of the industry's capacity to evolve and meet new challenges head-on. The integration of technology, the response to historical events, the impact of legislation, and the role of private firms in major events all highlight the dynamic nature of private security. Each development has contributed to a more sophisticated and effective approach to safeguarding people and assets, underscoring the continued relevance of private security in our daily lives.

Public vs. Private Policing: A Comparative Analysis

When you consider the roles of public and private policing, the distinctions are profound yet intricate. Public police forces operate under the jurisdictional authority granted by the state, allowing them to enforce laws, maintain order, and protect citizens' rights on a broad scale. Their responsibilities are deeply intertwined with public trust, making them the face of government authority on the streets.

In contrast, private security operates within the confines of contractual obligations, serving specific clients or properties. Their authority is limited to the premises they are hired to protect, and they lack the power to enforce laws beyond the scope of their contracts. This difference in jurisdiction underscores a fundamental disparity in how each entity functions within society.

Accountability and transparency are pivotal in assessing the effectiveness of policing. Public forces are subject to rigorous oversight by governmental bodies, media scrutiny, and public opinion, ensuring a level of transparency that is essential for maintaining public trust. Conversely, private security firms are accountable primarily to their employers, which can lead to varying standards of accountability and transparency. This raises questions about how these organizations handle sensitive situations, such as incidents involving the use of force or breaches of privacy. While public forces are bound by comprehensive regulations, private firms operate under a patchwork of industry standards and legal requirements that vary significantly by region.

The benefits and drawbacks of private policing are multifaceted. On one hand, private firms offer flexibility and responsiveness, characteristics that can be particularly valuable in rapidly changing environments. They can tailor their services to meet specific client needs, from corporate security to personal protection, without the bureaucratic constraints that often hamper public agencies. However, this flexibility comes with concerns regarding profit motives. When security is driven by profit, it raises ethical questions about who receives protection and at what cost. In this context, critics argue that this model could prioritize wealthier clients over the general public, potentially widening gaps in security and justice.

Legal and ethical implications are at the heart of the debate over private policing. Civil liberties concerns loom large, as private security personnel may not be held to the same constitutional standards as public officials. This disparity can lead to situations where privacy and personal freedoms are compromised, particularly in areas like surveillance and data collection. Ethical considerations also arise in profit-driven models, where the focus on financial gain may conflict with the ethical obligation to protect and serve impartially. The balance between business interests and ethical responsibilities is delicate and often contentious.

Case Study: Integrated Security Operations

Consider the relationship between the London Metropolitan Police and private security firms. This dynamic showcases both the potential and the challenges of collaboration. In urban centers like London, integrated security operations have become a necessity. Public forces and private firms often work side by side, combining resources and expertise to enhance safety. These partnerships can lead to improved outcomes, such as quicker response times and more comprehensive coverage of large events or high-risk areas. However, conflicts can arise when roles overlap or when communication breaks down. Thus, the key to successful collaboration lies in clear delineation of responsibilities and open channels of communication.

In essence, the interaction between public and private forces is a balancing act, requiring careful navigation of jurisdictional boundaries and ethical considerations. As we explore further, you'll conclude that the landscape of policing is one of constant negotiation, shaped by evolving societal needs and the relentless march of technology.

Private Policing and Urbanization: A Symbiotic Relationship

Urbanization has reshaped the landscape of cities across the globe, creating both opportunities and challenges that demand innovative solutions. As populations swell and dense urban centers become the norm, public police forces often find themselves stretched thin, struggling to meet the diverse demands of their communities.

This increased population density means more people are living, working, and interacting in close quarters, which can amplify the potential for conflict, crime, and disorder. Hence, the complexity of urban life requires a multifaceted approach to security, one that public police forces, with their limited resources, sometimes cannot provide. The sheer scale of modern cities can overwhelm traditional policing models, leading to gaps in coverage and response times, which create a fertile ground for private policing to step in and offer tailored solutions.

Private security firms have adeptly adapted to the unique challenges presented by urban environments. They leverage technology in ways that public forces often cannot, employing advanced surveillance systems that provide comprehensive monitoring over vast areas. This technological edge allows real-time data analysis, enabling swift decision-making and proactive measures. In cities where every second counts, the ability to rapidly deploy resources based on live information can make a significant difference in maintaining order and safety.

Moreover, private security firms often engage in community-based initiatives that foster trust and collaboration with local residents, including neighborhood patrols, community meetings, and partnerships with local businesses, all aimed at creating a sense of collective security and responsibility. By working closely with those they serve, private security agents can not only respond to incidents more effectively but also help prevent them.

Furthermore, the economic impact of robust private security is significant. Safe neighborhoods attract businesses, and businesses bring jobs, investment, and prosperity. In bustling business districts, the presence of private security can reduce crime rates, creating an environment where commerce can thrive. This reduction in crime not only protects assets but also enhances the quality of life for residents and visitors alike. Cities with effective security measures often see increased real estate values as both commercial and residential tenants seek the stability that comes with a secure environment. The economic benefits extend beyond immediate safety, cascading into broader economic development and community well-being. Security, therefore, becomes a critical component of urban planning and economic strategy, influencing everything from tourism to local business growth.

Collaboration between urban planners and private security firms is becoming increasingly common, as they work together to create environments that are not only functional but also secure. Public-private partnerships in urban design can lead to innovative solutions that integrate security into the very fabric of city planning. These partnerships can result in the strategic placement of surveillance infrastructure, the design of public spaces that enhances visibility and reduces crime opportunities, and the implementation of technologies that link public and private security networks.

In some cases, private security firms take the lead in urban redevelopment projects, investing in areas that have been neglected and transforming them into vibrant, secure communities. By prioritizing safety and security, these projects can revitalize neighborhoods, attract new residents and businesses, and contribute to the overall health and vitality of urban areas.

Interactive Element: Urban Security Checklist

Consider using an urban security checklist to assess the safety of your neighborhood or business district. This could include questions like:

- Are there visible security patrols in the area?

- Is there adequate lighting in public spaces?

- Are surveillance cameras in place and monitored?

- Do local businesses collaborate with security firms for additional safety measures?

Reflect on these aspects to better understand the security landscape of your environment.

The symbiotic relationship between private policing and urbanization is evident in the way cities evolve and adapt to new challenges. As urban environments continue to grow and change, the role of private security will likely expand, offering innovative solutions that complement and enhance public efforts. The interplay between these forces is dynamic, reflecting the ever-changing needs of urban populations and the critical importance of security in fostering thriving, sustainable cities.

Understanding the Private Security Market: Key Players and Trends

In the vast arena of private security, certain players dominate the field, shaping its direction and evolution. G4S stands out among these giants, boasting an international reach that spans across continents. With operations in over 90 countries, G4S provides a range of services from securing airports and ports to protecting government buildings and private properties. This global presence allows G4S to leverage local knowledge while maintaining a consistent standard of service, adapting its strategies to regional needs and regulations. The firm's ability to operate at such a scale demonstrates the increasing globalization of security services, where local expertise is coupled with international resources.

On the other hand, Securitas AB, a Swedish company, employs a more focused market strategy, emphasizing specialized services and local adaptability. By tailoring its security solutions to meet specific market demands, Securitas distinguishes itself through its expertise in areas like fire protection, mobile patrols, and electronic surveillance. The firm's approach highlights the importance of understanding and responding to unique client needs, which has proven essential in maintaining its competitive edge.

As the private security industry continues to evolve, several trends are emerging that redefine its landscape. A significant shift is the growth of cybersecurity services, a response to the expanding digital threats facing businesses and individuals alike. With the proliferation of cyberattacks, private security firms have diversified their offerings to include protection against digital intrusions, emphasizing the need for a comprehensive approach to security that blends physical and cyber solutions. This trend is fueled by the increasing reliance on digital infrastructure, which presents both opportunities and challenges for security providers.

In parallel, there is a noticeable rise in boutique security firms. These smaller companies offer highly specialized services, often catering to niche markets that require tailored solutions. Unlike their larger counterparts, boutique firms can provide personalized attention and customized strategies, appealing to clients who seek more than just generic security solutions. This rise signifies a shift toward more individualized service offerings in the industry, as clients demand solutions that address specific vulnerabilities.

On the other hand, economic forces significantly shape the private security market, with globalization and technological advancements leading the charge. The global economy's fluctuations impact the demand for security services, as periods of economic uncertainty often spur increased investment in protection measures. Businesses and individuals alike seek to safeguard their assets in times of instability, driving growth in the security sector.

Furthermore, technological advancements have revolutionized the way security is conducted. The integration of cutting-edge technologies, such as AI and IoT, into security operations has transformed traditional practices, offering more efficient and effective ways to protect assets. These advancements not only enhance the capabilities of security firms but also create new avenues for growth and innovation. Companies that can effectively harness these technologies position themselves as leaders in a rapidly evolving market.

Within this competitive landscape, private security firms strive to differentiate themselves through service diversification and brand reputation management. By offering a broad range of services, from traditional guarding to advanced electronic monitoring, they can meet the diverse needs of their clients, ensuring that they remain relevant in a dynamic market. This diversification allows companies to tap into multiple revenue streams, mitigating risks associated with market fluctuations.

Equally important is the management of brand reputation. In an industry where trust is paramount, firms invest heavily in building and maintaining a positive image. This involves not only delivering high-quality services but also adhering to ethical standards and demonstrating social responsibility. A strong reputation can be a decisive factor for clients when choosing a security provider, underscoring the importance of transparency and reliability in building long-term relationships.

As we navigate the complexities of the private security market, these players and trends reveal an industry in constant flux, driven by innovation and adaptation. The interplay of global forces, technological progress, and client demands shapes a market that is both challenging and full of potential.

The Global Expansion of Private Policing: Cultural and Economic Influences

Private policing is not only a product of local needs but also a reflection of cultural attitudes and economic realities. In the United States, private security is deeply embedded in the cultural fabric, often viewed as a necessary supplement to public law enforcement. The vastness of the country, coupled with a strong emphasis on individualism and personal responsibility, has fostered a culture where private security is both accepted and expected. Americans tend to value the autonomy and specialized services that private firms offer, from gated communities to corporate headquarters. This acceptance is mirrored in the sheer size of the industry, with the US boasting one of the largest private security workforces in the world.

In contrast, Europe approaches private security with a more regulated framework. European nations often prioritize stringent oversight, emphasizing the role of private security as complementary to public forces rather than a replacement. Regulatory bodies, such as those established by the European Union, ensure that private security services adhere to strict standards, reflecting a cultural commitment to maintaining a balance between security and civil liberties.

Economic factors play a major role in the global expansion of private policing. In emerging markets, rapid economic growth often outpaces the development of public infrastructure, including law enforcement. This creates a demand for private security to fill the gaps left by underfunded or understaffed public forces. Countries experiencing economic liberalization frequently experience a surge in private investment, leading to increased demand for security services to protect these new assets.

Globalization also contributes to the expansion of private security as multinational corporations seek to safeguard their interests across borders. This demand drives the growth of international security firms, which capitalize on the need for consistent security standards in diverse economic environments. As a result, private security becomes not just a local necessity but a global business that caters to the complexities of a connected world.

Multinational security firms play a pivotal role in this global market, leveraging their vast networks and expertise to operate across different jurisdictions. These firms engage in cross-border operations, providing a range of services that include risk assessment, asset protection, and crisis management. By forming local partnerships and collaborations, they can tailor their services to meet specific regional needs while maintaining the high standards expected by their international clientele. This strategic approach allows them to navigate the intricacies of local regulations and cultural expectations, which positions them as key players in the global security landscape. The ability of these firms to adapt and integrate into local markets underscores their influence and importance in the broader context of international security.

On the other hand, global challenges have a profound impact on private policing, reshaping priorities and strategies. The COVID-19 pandemic, for example, highlighted the need for adaptable security solutions, as traditional methods were disrupted by lockdowns and social distancing measures. Private security firms quickly adapted by implementing health protocols, managing access to facilities, and ensuring compliance with rapidly changing regulations. In conflict zones, private security often fills the void left by inadequate public forces, providing protection for humanitarian efforts, businesses, and individuals. These firms employ specialized strategies to operate in high-risk environments, balancing the need for security with the complexities of local dynamics. The ongoing evolution of security needs in response to global challenges underscores the flexibility and resilience of private policing.

The narrative of private policing is one of adaptation and growth, shaped by the interplay of cultural perceptions and economic forces. As societies evolve, so does the role of private security, reflecting the changing priorities and challenges of a globalized world. This expansion is not without its complexities, as it navigates the delicate balance between public trust and private enterprise.

The patterns and practices observed across different regions offer valuable insights into how private policing can effectively complement public efforts, providing security solutions that are both innovative and responsive to the needs of diverse communities. As we conclude this exploration, it is clear that the future of private policing will continue to be defined by its ability to adapt to the ever-changing dynamics of global security.

Chapter 2:

Legal Frameworks and Ethical

Considerations

Imagine a world where the rules governing private policing are as varied as the landscapes across the globe. The legal frameworks that underpin private security services are not only complex but also critical in ensuring accountability and transparency. For college students and policymakers, understanding these frameworks is vital, as they shape the very environments in which security operations occur.

Private security does not operate in a vacuum; it is bound by laws that dictate everything from the contracts to the liabilities. This chapter will guide you through these complexities, offering a road map to address the legal intricacies of private policing.

Navigating Complex Legal Frameworks: A Step-By-Step Guide

At the heart of private security operations are the foundational legal principles that guide their actions. These principles are grounded in contract law, which forms the backbone of security agreements. In this setting, contracts define the scope of services, responsibilities, and expectations between clients and security providers. They are meticulously crafted to ensure clarity and prevent disputes, outlining everything from the duration of services to the specific tasks security personnel are authorized to perform. Liability issues further compound these agreements, as private security firms must navigate potential legal repercussions associated with their operations. Whether it's a breach of contract or an incident involving the use of force, understanding liability is essential for both legal compliance and risk management.

If you're entering the field of private security, obtaining the necessary licenses and permits is a necessary step. The process can be daunting, as it varies significantly depending on the jurisdiction. In the United States, for instance, licensing requirements differ not only from one state to another but also within different municipalities. According to the 50-State Security Licensing Compliance Guide, most states impose licensing requirements on both individuals and the company as a whole. This ensures that all personnel meet certain educational and professional standards before they are legally allowed to operate. Compliance with these regulations is not just a legal obligation; it's a commitment to maintaining high professional standards, which reassures clients of the firm's credibility and authority. Meeting these requirements involves understanding the specific criteria set by state boards, which may include background checks, examinations, and continuing education and training.

Jurisdictional variations play a key role in shaping legal requirements for private security. In the United States, the contrast between state and federal regulations can complicate operations for companies that work across multiple states. Each state may have its own set of laws governing security practices, from firearm qualifications to the necessity of registering as a private investigator. The European Union presents its own challenges, with member states adhering to a combination of EU-wide directives and national regulations. This mosaic of laws requires firms to be vigilant, ensuring compliance with all applicable legal standards. On the other hand, for policymakers, understanding these variations is essential when crafting legislation that can adapt to the diverse regulatory landscapes.

To effectively manage the legal risks associated with private policing, a robust legal risk assessment and management strategy is indispensable. This involves conducting *legal audits*, "a process that examines all aspects of a firm's operations to identify potential legal vulnerabilities." Audits help ensure compliance with applicable laws, assess the adequacy of contracts, and review liability exposure. Risk management frameworks further support these efforts by providing structured approaches to mitigate identified risks. They may include establishing protocols for incident reporting, implementing regular training programs, and creating comprehensive policies for data protection. By proactively addressing these risks, security firms can minimize legal disputes and enhance their overall operational integrity.

Interactive Element: Legal Compliance Checklist

Consider using a legal compliance checklist tailored for private security operations. It might include items such as verifying all personnel licenses, ensuring contracts are up to date, confirming adherence to local and national regulations, and maintaining documentation of training sessions. Reflecting on these aspects can help you gain a clearer understanding of the legal environment in which private security operates.

Furthermore, understanding the legal frameworks of private policing is not only about compliance; it's about foresight, preparation, and commitment to ethical practices. As you explore these principles, you'll find that navigating the legal landscape is a dynamic process, one that requires continuous adaptation to new laws and societal expectations.

Regulatory Challenges in Private Security: A Global Perspective

Understanding the regulatory landscape of private security on a global scale presents a unique set of challenges. Certification and training requirements stand out as primary hurdles for private security firms. These requirements vary significantly across regions, often reflecting local priorities and expectations. For example, in many U.S. states, security personnel must meet specific training hours and pass background checks to receive certification. Such standards ensure that they possess the necessary skills to perform their duties effectively. Yet, the disparity in training requirements can lead to inconsistencies in the quality of services provided by private firms across different jurisdictions.

Likewise, data protection and privacy laws have become increasingly stringent, especially in regions like the European Union. The General Data Protection Regulation (GDPR) has set a high bar for data privacy, requiring companies to justify their data collection practices and ensure consumer rights are protected. For private security firms, this means implementing robust data management systems and ensuring their operations comply with these regulations, which can be resource-intensive and complex.

On a higher level, international regulations, such as the GDPR, have far-reaching impacts on private security operations, extending beyond the borders of the EU. U.S.-based security companies, for instance, must adhere to these regulations when dealing with European clients or managing data related to EU citizens. This globalization of regulatory standards requires firms to maintain a keen awareness of international laws and adapt their practices accordingly.

Additionally, international security certifications, like ISO standards, play a critical role in shaping local security practices. These certifications establish benchmarks for quality and safety, helping firms demonstrate their commitment to high standards. Hence, obtaining such certifications can enhance a firm's reputation and competitiveness in the global market, but it also demands substantial investment in compliance and continuous improvement initiatives.

Professional organizations and industry bodies wield considerable influence in shaping the regulations that govern private security. ASIS International, for example, has been instrumental in developing standards and guidelines that promote the best practices across the industry. Their work helps unify disparate regulations and provides a framework for consistent security operations. In the UK, the Security Industry Authority (SIA) plays a similar role, setting licensing and training standards to ensure the competence and reliability of security personnel. These organizations not only advocate for their members' interests but also collaborate with government entities to craft policies that balance security needs with public safety and privacy concerns. Their contributions are vital in facing the complex regulatory environment and ensuring that private security operates with integrity and accountability.

The repercussions of failing to comply with regulatory standards can be severe. Noncompliance can result in hefty fines and legal penalties, which can cripple a firm's finances and disrupt operations. Beyond the immediate financial impact, the reputational damage from regulatory breaches can be even more detrimental. Clients and the public may lose trust in a firm that fails to adhere to established standards, leading to a decline in business and potential loss of contracts. In an industry where trust and reliability are paramount, maintaining compliance with regulations is not just a legal obligation but a necessary component of sustainable success. Thus, firms must invest in robust compliance programs and stay informed about regulatory changes to mitigate these risks.

Visual Element: Regulatory Compliance Infographic

Consider creating an infographic that outlines the key steps for achieving regulatory compliance in the private security industry. This visual guide could include stages, such as:

1. Understanding local and international regulations

2. Implementing data protection measures

3. Obtaining necessary certifications

4. Regularly reviewing compliance policies

Such a resource can serve as a quick reference for security firms striving to meet regulatory standards and maintain operational integrity.

Ethical Dilemmas in Privatized Policing: Balancing Profit and Public Good

In the world of private policing, the pursuit of profit often collides with ethical responsibilities, creating a tension that can be challenging to encounter. Imagine a security firm tasked with protecting a high-profile client. The client's interests may occasionally conflict with broader public safety concerns, raising questions about whose needs should take precedence. This conflict of interest is not uncommon in client relationships within the private security industry. When a firm's primary loyalty is to its paying client, the ethical lines can blur, particularly when the client's demands might undermine public welfare. Subsequently, security firms must carefully balance their contractual obligations with a commitment to ethical standards that protect the public good.

Resource allocation further complicates this ethical landscape. Consider a scenario where a private security company is contracted to secure a private estate in a high-crime neighborhood. The firm might allocate considerable resources to protect its client, potentially at the expense of wider community safety. This disparity raises questions about the equitable distribution of security resources and the role of private entities in contributing to public safety. The ethical challenge lies in ensuring that private security services do not exacerbate existing inequalities but instead work toward enhancing overall community well-being. Addressing this issue requires a thoughtful approach that considers both private and public interests.

In light of the aforementioned, ethical transparency is a cornerstone of responsible private policing. Clear ethical guidelines are essential to confirm that security operations are conducted with integrity and accountability. In this context, establishing an ethical code of conduct provides a framework for decision-making, guiding security personnel in situations where moral dilemmas arise.

Transparency in operations and decision-making processes fosters trust among clients, employees, and the communities they serve. When security firms openly communicate their practices and prioritize ethical standards, they not only enhance their reputation but also contribute to a culture of accountability within the industry.

Corporate social responsibility (CSR) represents another avenue through which private security firms can contribute positively to society. By engaging in community initiatives, these companies can build stronger relationships with the neighborhoods they serve, thereby enhancing public trust and cooperation. Such initiatives might include supporting local youth programs, providing security consultations for community events, or partnering with local law enforcement to address specific safety concerns.

Additionally, environmental sustainability practices offer an opportunity for security firms to demonstrate their commitment to broader societal well-being. Implementing eco-friendly practices, such as reducing energy consumption in surveillance systems or utilizing green transportation for patrols, can position firms as leaders in sustainable business practices.

Additionally, resolving ethical conflicts requires a proactive approach, utilizing frameworks that support ethical decision-making. Models such as the Ethical Decision-Making Framework provide structured processes for evaluating options and identifying the most ethical course of action in complex situations. These models encourage security personnel to consider the potential impact of their decisions on all stakeholders involved, promoting a holistic approach to ethical challenges.

Moreover, implementing whistleblower protection policies is essential in fostering an environment where employees feel empowered to report unethical behavior without fear of retaliation. Such policies guarantee that ethical breaches are addressed promptly, reinforcing the firm's commitment to upholding high ethical standards.

Textual Element: Ethical Decision-Making Scenario

Consider an ethical decision-making scenario where a security firm is contracted to protect a private corporation suspected of unethical environmental practices. Reflect on how the firm might deal with this situation, considering the impact of its actions on public perception and community trust. Would the firm prioritize client confidentiality or engage with local stakeholders to address community concerns? Reflect on the potential outcomes of each approach and consider the role of ethical guidelines in driving the firm's decision-making process.

Case Law and Private Security: Key Judicial Decisions

In the realm of private security, landmark legal cases have played a major role in shaping operational practices and establishing legal precedents. These cases often serve as the foundation for understanding liability and the use of force within the industry. One of the most notable cases in security liability is Wade v. Byles, where the court ruled that private security guards, like Oscar Byles, who was involved in an altercation while on duty, were not state actors under the United States Constitution. This case illustrated that even though private security personnel may perform functions similar to public police, they do not inherently assume the same legal responsibilities. It highlighted the distinct separation between private and public law enforcement, emphasizing the need for clear contractual agreements and operational boundaries within private security firms.

The implications of such rulings extend beyond the courtroom, influencing the way private security companies draft contracts and train their employees. This case serves as a constant reminder that while private security personnel may act in capacities akin to public officers, their legal standing remains separate, affecting how liability is managed within the industry.

Judicial rulings have also highly impacted the protocols surrounding the use of force by private security personnel. In various cases, courts have scrutinized the actions of security guards, determining whether their use of force was justified under the circumstances. These decisions have set precedents that influence current training programs, ensuring that security personnel understand the legal boundaries of their authority. For instance, when courts evaluate whether a security guard's actions were reasonable, they often consider factors such as the perceived threat level and the response's proportionality. This legal scrutiny underscores the importance of comprehensive training that equips security personnel with the skills to assess situations accurately and respond appropriately. As a result, private security firms have adapted their training curricula to incorporate these legal standards, emphasizing de-escalation techniques and clear decision-making protocols.

Case law is not static; it evolves as courts interpret existing laws and address new legal challenges. As legal interpretations change over time, so too do the operational guidelines for private security firms. In this context, appeals play a key role in shaping case law, often leading to revised interpretations that reflect contemporary societal values and legal principles. For private security firms, staying informed about these changes is vital. Adjustments in security policies may be necessary to align with new legal expectations, ensuring compliance and minimizing liability risks. This dynamic nature of legal frameworks requires ongoing vigilance and adaptation by security firms, as they must continuously evaluate and update their operational protocols to reflect the latest legal developments.

In practical terms, the influence of case law on daily operations is profound. Security firms often implement changes in response to judicial rulings, adjusting policies to mitigate risks and ensure compliance. For example, a court ruling that emphasizes the importance of clear communication during security incidents might prompt a firm to revise its communication protocols, confirming that all personnel are trained to articulate their actions effectively.

Additionally, training programs often incorporate case law scenarios to provide security personnel with hands-on experience in addressing complex legal situations. These scenarios help personnel understand the implications of judicial decisions, reinforcing the importance of adhering to legal standards in their daily duties.

Textual Element: Case Law Scenario Exercise

Consider a scenario exercise where you are a security manager tasked with revising the use-of-force policy after a recent court ruling. Reflect on the key elements that need to be addressed to align with the legal precedent. How would you ensure all personnel understand and implement the new guidelines? This exercise can help you appreciate the practical application of case law in shaping security operations.

Ethical Compliance in Private Policing: Standards and Practices

Ethical compliance is the cornerstone of trust and integrity in private policing. As private security firms navigate complex operational environments, adherence to international ethical standards becomes vital. The Voluntary Principles on Security and Human Rights offer a framework for integrating human rights into security practices, guiding firms in conducting risk assessments and guaranteeing their operations respect fundamental freedoms. These principles emphasize the importance of transparency and accountability, encouraging companies to engage with local communities and stakeholders in meaningful dialogue.

Similarly, the International Code of Conduct for Private Security Providers (ICoC) sets forth comprehensive guidelines for private security operations, focusing on the protection of human rights and the prevention of abuses. By aligning with these international benchmarks, private security firms not only demonstrate their commitment to ethical practices but also enhance their legitimacy and credibility in a globalized market.

Maintaining ethical standards in private policing requires proactive strategies and robust systems. Developing comprehensive ethics training programs is one such strategy that equips security personnel with the knowledge and skills to face ethical dilemmas in their daily operations. These programs should encompass a wide range of scenarios, from handling conflicts of interest to respecting client confidentiality, which ensures personnel are well-prepared for the ethical challenges they may face. Regular ethical audits and assessments further support this effort, providing a mechanism for continuous improvement and accountability. By routinely evaluating their practices and identifying areas for enhancement, firms can maintain high ethical standards and address any potential lapses before they escalate into dangerous issues.

Leadership plays a pivotal role in fostering an ethical culture within private security firms. Ethical leadership begins with accountability, as leaders must be willing to take responsibility for ethical breaches and commit to corrective action. This accountability sets the tone for the entire organization, signaling that ethical conduct is a priority and that deviations will not be tolerated. Additionally, senior management must serve as role models for ethical behavior, demonstrating transparency and integrity in their actions. By embodying these values, leaders inspire their teams to uphold ethical standards and create an environment where ethical considerations are integrated into decision-making processes at every level.

The impact of ethical compliance on a business's reputation is profound. In an industry where trust is paramount, maintaining high ethical standards builds confidence among clients and stakeholders. When security firms consistently demonstrate ethical behavior, they cultivate strong relationships with their clients, who are reassured by the firm's commitment to integrity and transparency. This trust not only enhances client satisfaction but also fosters long-term partnerships, contributing to the firm's stability and growth.

Furthermore, a solid ethical reputation enhances brand competitiveness in the marketplace. In a field where competition is fierce, firms recognized for their ethical practices often stand out, attracting new clients and retaining existing ones. This reputation can be a decisive factor for clients when selecting a security provider, underscoring the value of ethical compliance as a strategic asset.

Human Rights in Private Security Operations

Incorporating human rights considerations into security practices is not just a legal obligation; it is a moral imperative. As private security grows, so does the need to ensure that operations respect the dignity and rights of individuals. Human rights impact assessments serve as a necessary tool in this endeavor. They evaluate how security policies and practices affect human rights, identifying potential risks and areas for improvement. By integrating these assessments into their operations, security firms can proactively address issues before they escalate, confirming that their practices align with both legal standards and societal values.

Embedding human rights into security policies involves crafting guidelines that prioritize the protection of individual freedoms. Policies must be explicit in their commitment to human rights, incorporating principles that safeguard against abuses. This integration requires a thorough understanding of both the legal landscape and the ethical considerations that underpin human rights. Security personnel should be trained to recognize and confront situations where rights might be at stake, ensuring their actions enhance rather than undermine public safety. The challenge lies in balancing these rights with the necessity of maintaining security, especially in contexts where tensions run high.

Surveillance technologies illustrate the delicate balance between security and privacy. While these tools offer a powerful means of preventing crime and ensuring safety, they also pose significant risks to individual privacy. The deployment of cameras and data collection systems must be carefully managed to avoid infringing on personal rights. This involves setting clear boundaries on data use, making sure surveillance practices are transparent, and providing individuals with the ability to challenge or inquire about the use of their data. In high-risk environments, where the need for security is most acute, the challenge intensifies. Subsequently, security measures must be robust enough to protect assets and people yet sensitive to the rights of those involved.

International frameworks provide a foundation for integrating human rights into private security operations. The UN Guiding Principles on Business and Human Rights offer a global standard, urging companies to respect human rights in their operations and supply chains. These principles emphasize the responsibility of businesses to prevent and address human rights abuses, providing a framework for accountability. Similarly, the Montreux Document on Private Military and Security Companies outlines the best practices and legal obligations for private security contractors, reinforcing the importance of operating within the bounds of international law. These documents serve as valuable resources for security firms seeking to align their practices with global standards.

The successful integration of human rights into security practices is demonstrated in various case studies. Community-based security initiatives often lead the way in respecting local rights while enhancing safety. For instance, security firms that engage with community leaders and residents to tailor their services see improved outcomes. These initiatives foster trust, allowing security personnel to work effectively within the community while respecting local customs and expectations. Collaboration with nongovernmental organizations (NGOs) further exemplifies how private security can support human rights. By partnering with NGOs, security firms can gain valuable insights into human rights issues and work collaboratively to address them. These partnerships can lead to innovative solutions that balance security needs with the protection of rights.

As you explore the role of human rights in private security, consider the broader implications of these practices. Balancing security with respect for human rights is not merely a regulatory requirement; it is a reflection of values and commitments in a society. The integration of human rights into security operations challenges firms to think critically about their impact on individuals and communities. It also emphasizes the need for ongoing dialogue and adaptation to ensure that security practices evolve in response to changing societal expectations.

As we move forward, the principles and practices highlighted in this chapter will continue to shape the future of private security, influencing how we define and pursue safety in a complex world. As we close this chapter, it's clear that the intertwining of security and human rights is vital for meaningful progress. In the subsequent chapter, we'll explore how technology is reshaping private security, offering new tools and challenges for those committed to protecting both people and rights.

Chapter 3:

Technology and Innovation in Private Security

Consider a world where every action is captured, every movement tracked, and every piece of data analyzed. This isn't science fiction; it's the reality of modern surveillance. As you read this chapter, you'll explore the profound impact of surveillance systems on private security, a topic that resonates deeply with both students and policymakers.

The Rise of Digital Surveillance

The evolution of surveillance has been a journey from rudimentary observation to sophisticated digital ecosystems. Back in the day, early CCTV systems were nothing more than crude setups, capturing grainy black-and-white footage on looped tapes. Yet, these systems laid the groundwork for what was to come, providing a sense of security that was unprecedented at the time. They represented a leap forward in crime prevention, offering a stationary eye that never blinked.

As technology advanced, so did the capabilities of surveillance systems. The transition from analog to digital marked a turning point, ushering in an era of networked surveillance where cameras became interconnected information hubs. This shift was not merely about improving image quality; it was about creating systems that could communicate, analyze, and respond in real-time.

Digital surveillance brought the power of data, allowing for sophisticated analytics and pattern recognition. These systems could now track not just individuals but trends, offering insights into behavior and potential threats before they materialized. This level of oversight transformed security operations, making them more proactive and less reliant on human intervention.

But with great power comes great responsibility, and the dual role of surveillance as both a security tool and a privacy concern cannot be overstated. On one hand, surveillance can deter crime, providing a watchful presence that discourages unlawful behavior. On the other hand, it raises notable questions about privacy and the extent to which individuals are monitored. The public's concern over constant monitoring is valid, as the line between safety and intrusion often blurs.

Furthermore, legal implications abound, with privacy laws struggling to keep pace with technological advancements. Policymakers grapple with crafting regulations that protect individual rights without stifling innovation and security effectiveness. Balancing these interests requires a nuanced approach, one that respects privacy while acknowledging the benefits of surveillance in maintaining public safety.

Surveillance's effectiveness in crime prevention is backed by compelling evidence. Case studies from urban centers demonstrate significant reductions in crime rates when visible surveillance is in place. In neighborhoods where cameras are installed, data show a marked decrease in incidents of theft and vandalism. The mere presence of cameras acts as a deterrent, signaling that someone is watching and that criminal acts are less likely to go unnoticed. This deterrent effect is particularly pronounced in high-traffic areas, where the likelihood of being caught on camera is high. Yet, it's important to recognize that surveillance is not a panacea. Its success is contingent on proper implementation and integration with broader security strategies.

The regulatory frameworks governing surveillance use play a pivotal role in shaping how these systems are deployed. Privacy laws, such as those in the European Union, set stringent standards for data protection, ensuring that surveillance practices do not infringe upon individual rights. These laws mandate transparency, requiring that individuals are informed about surveillance practices and that their data are handled with care.

Guidelines for ethical surveillance practices emphasize the need for accountability and oversight, urging companies to implement measures that prevent abuse and ensure compliance. For policymakers, the challenge lies in crafting regulations that are robust, adaptable, and capable of addressing the rapid pace of technological change.

Visual Element: Surveillance System Infographic

Consider an infographic that illustrates the evolution of surveillance systems, from early CCTV setups to modern digital networks. This visual guide could highlight key milestones, technological advancements, and their impact on privacy and security. By examining these elements, you can gain a deeper understanding of how surveillance has transformed over time and its implications for the future of security.

Cybersecurity in Private Policing: Protecting Digital Borders

In today's digital age, the role of cybersecurity in private policing extends far beyond traditional security measures. It's not only about safeguarding physical spaces but also about protecting digital assets that are equally vulnerable to threats. Therefore, private policing firms must now defend confidential client data, which, if compromised, can lead to significant reputational and financial damage. This protection involves securing sensitive information such as personal identification, financial records, and proprietary business data, ensuring that only authorized individuals have access.

Internal communications within a security firm are also paramount, as they often contain strategic plans and sensitive information that, if leaked, could compromise operations. Safeguarding these communications from prying eyes is vital to maintaining operational integrity and client trust.

The landscape of cyber threats that private security firms face is vast and ever-evolving. Among the most prevalent threats are *phishing* attacks, where "malicious actors attempt to trick individuals into revealing sensitive information through deceptive emails or messages." These attacks can lead to unauthorized access to systems and data breaches. In addition, *social engineering attacks*, which "manipulate individuals into divulging confidential information," pose a significant risk as well. Additionally, ransomware incidents have become increasingly common, where attackers encrypt a firm's data and demand a ransom for their release. Such attacks not only disrupt operations but can also lead to dangerous financial losses and damage to a firm's reputation. Understanding these threats is crucial for developing effective defense strategies.

Implementing robust cybersecurity measures is essential for mitigating these threats and protecting digital borders. One of the most effective strategies is the adoption of multifactor authentication systems. This adds an extra layer of security by requiring users to verify their identity through multiple methods, such as a password and a fingerprint scan.

Moreover, regular cybersecurity training for staff is paramount. By educating employees about potential threats and safe practices, firms can reduce the risk of human error, which is often the weakest link in cybersecurity defenses. This training should be ongoing, as cyber threats are constantly evolving, and staying informed is key to maintaining a strong security posture.

Cybersecurity doesn't operate in isolation; it is an integral part of a comprehensive security strategy. Digital security measures complement physical security by ensuring that access controls are not only in place but also fortified by technology. For instance, integrating cybersecurity protocols with physical access controls can prevent unauthorized entry into secure areas, both physically and digitally. Collaborative cyber-physical security strategies involve combining efforts across various security domains to create a cohesive defense mechanism. This approach ensures that all potential vulnerabilities are addressed, providing a comprehensive protective shield for clients and assets alike.

Interactive Element: Cyber Threat Awareness Quiz

Consider taking a cyber threat awareness quiz to test your understanding of common cyber threats and best protection practices. This quiz might include questions about identifying phishing emails, understanding the importance of multifactor authentication, and recognizing the signs of ransomware attacks. Reflecting on your responses can help reinforce your knowledge and highlight areas where further education may be beneficial.

The Impact of Artificial Intelligence on Private Security Operations

Artificial Intelligence (AI) has revolutionized private security operations, offering capabilities once considered the realm of science fiction. At the forefront of this transformation is AI-driven video analytics, which allows systems to process and interpret vast amounts of video data with remarkable precision. These advanced algorithms can identify unusual patterns or behaviors in real-time, alerting security personnel to potential threats before they escalate. For instance, AI can detect when someone leaves a bag unattended or when a vehicle is parked in a restricted area, enabling rapid response. This technology reduces the need for constant human monitoring, freeing up personnel for more complex tasks. Machine learning algorithms further enhance threat detection by continuously learning from data. They adapt to new patterns, becoming more accurate over time. This adaptability is vital in environments where threats are constantly evolving, helping security teams stay one step ahead.

The benefits of AI in private security extend beyond mere detection. AI significantly enhances efficiency across operations. Automating routine monitoring tasks frees up human resources, allowing personnel to focus on strategic decision-making. Instead of sifting through hours of footage, security teams can rely on AI to pinpoint the moments that matter.

Predictive analytics, another AI application, empowers security teams to anticipate threats. By analyzing historical data, AI models can identify patterns that precede security incidents, enabling proactive measures. For example, if data indicate an increase in security breaches during specific times, teams can adjust their strategies accordingly. This proactive approach not only improves response times but also minimizes the risk of incidents.

However, the use of AI in security is not without ethical challenges. Concerns about bias in AI algorithms are paramount, as these systems may inadvertently perpetuate existing prejudices present in the data they learn from. If an AI system is trained on biased data, it may disproportionately target certain groups, leading to unfair treatment and potential legal repercussions. Ensuring diversity in training data and implementing rigorous testing protocols can help mitigate these risks.

Transparency in AI-driven security decisions is equally important. Security firms must ensure that their AI systems operate transparently, with clear explanations provided for automated decisions. This transparency fosters trust among stakeholders and ensures accountability. Stakeholders, be they clients or the public, should have insight into how AI systems make decisions, particularly when these decisions impact individual rights.

Real-world applications of AI in private security provide compelling evidence of its potential. Consider AI-enhanced perimeter security systems, which leverage AI to monitor and secure large areas efficiently. In these systems, AI analyzes data from sensors and cameras to detect intrusions, even in challenging weather or lighting conditions. This capability is invaluable for securing critical infrastructure, such as airports and power plants, where breaches can have severe consequences. Another notable application is the use of facial recognition technologies in corporate security. These systems can identify individuals in real-time, granting or denying access based on preset criteria. While effective, these technologies also raise privacy concerns, emphasizing the need for careful implementation and oversight. The use of facial recognition can streamline access control, enhancing both security and convenience. However, it must be balanced with respect for privacy, ensuring data are used responsibly and with consent.

Textual Element: AI Implementation Case Study

Consider a case study involving AI deployment in a large-scale stadium security operation. In this setting, AI is used to monitor crowd behavior, identifying potential security threats before they materialize. AI-driven analytics detect anomalies, such as a sudden gathering of people in restricted areas, allowing security teams to respond swiftly. This proactive approach enhances safety and ensures a seamless experience for attendees.

Reflect on the implications of such technology, considering both its security benefits and ethical considerations.

Drones and Robotics in Security: The Future of Private Policing

The use of drones and robotics in security operations represents a significant leap forward in the capabilities of private policing. If you picture the traditional security guard patrolling a perimeter, imagine replacing or augmenting that presence with drones zipping through the air and robots rolling along the ground.

Drones, equipped with high-definition cameras and sensors, extend surveillance capabilities far beyond the limitations of human observation. They can cover large areas quickly, providing real-time data and a bird's-eye view that enhances situational awareness. This technology is particularly useful in monitoring vast or remote locations where human patrols may be impractical or too slow to respond to fast-moving situations.

Meanwhile, robotic patrol units are increasingly being deployed in urban environments, navigating through crowds or working alongside humans to monitor safety. These robots can be equipped with sensors that detect anomalies, such as unauthorized access or unusual environmental changes, alerting human operators to potential threats.

Yet, while drones and robotics offer impressive enhancements to security operations, they are not without limitations. The most apparent advantage is their ability to extend surveillance reach, providing comprehensive coverage that would be challenging or impossible for human teams alone. However, this increased reach comes with technical challenges. Drones require skilled operators and are subject to weather conditions that can limit their effectiveness. They also demand regular maintenance to remain operational, which can be costly and time-consuming.

Similarly, robotic units need to navigate complex environments, requiring sophisticated programming and the ability to adapt to unforeseen obstacles. Maintenance issues, like sensor malfunctions or battery failures, can hinder their performance, highlighting the need for continuous technological improvements and robust support systems.

The deployment of drones and robotics in security is also heavily regulated, subjecting them to a variety of legal and operational constraints. Drones, for instance, must comply with aviation regulations that govern airspace usage, which are designed to prevent collisions and ensure the safe integration of drones into the skies; however, they can also limit where and how drones can be used. Understanding and adhering to these rules is required for security firms wishing to utilize drones effectively. Furthermore, safety standards for robotic operations are critical to prevent accidents, especially in crowded or sensitive environments. Robotics must adhere to protocols that ensure they do not pose a risk to humans or property, which involves regular testing and compliance with industry standards.

Despite these challenges, innovative uses of drones and robotics continue to emerge, showcasing their potential in various security scenarios. One exciting application is automated crowd monitoring at large events, such as concerts or sports matches. Drones can hover above the crowd, scanning for disturbances or emergencies, while robots patrol the perimeters, offering assistance or directing attendees.

Moreover, in hazardous environments, robotics provides invaluable support, taking on tasks too dangerous for humans. For instance, robots can enter areas with toxic spills, explosive threats, or unstable structures, assessing risks and gathering critical data without endangering human lives. These applications highlight the transformative potential of drones and robotics in security as they continue to expand the horizons of what is possible in private policing.

Biometric Technologies: Revolutionizing Identification in Security

Imagine entering a building without the need for keys or access cards simply by letting a scanner recognize your face or fingerprint. This seamless experience is at the heart of biometric technologies, which have reshaped the landscape of security identification. Biometric systems use unique physiological characteristics, such as fingerprints, irises, and facial features, to verify identity.

Fingerprint recognition systems, one of the earliest forms, offer a reliable identification method. They analyze the unique patterns of ridges and valleys on a fingertip, enabling secure access that passwords can't simply match. Iris recognition takes this a step further by examining the intricate patterns in the colored part of the eye. Known for its high accuracy, it's often used in high-security environments where precision is nonnegotiable. Additionally, facial recognition technology, while more recent, has rapidly gained traction. It captures an image of a person's face and maps the unique geometry, comparing it to a stored database. This technology has found its way into smartphones, airports, and even law enforcement, offering a convenient and efficient means of identification.

The advantages of biometric systems extend beyond convenience; they enhance security by ensuring that only authorized individuals gain access to protected areas. In this context, streamlined access control systems benefit from biometric integration, reducing the need for physical keys or cards that can be lost or stolen. Instead, individuals simply use their unique biological traits as keys, which are much harder to duplicate or forge. This not only improves security but also enhances the user experience by eliminating the hassle associated with traditional access methods. Similarly, enhanced identity verification procedures benefit from biometrics by providing a fast and accurate way to confirm identities. This is particularly beneficial in high-traffic areas like airports, where speed and accuracy are paramount. By using biometric data, security personnel can quickly and confidently verify the identity of travelers, ensuring smooth and secure operations.

However, with great power comes great responsibility, and the use of biometrics raises significant privacy and ethical concerns. Data storage and management present challenges, as biometric data are sensitive and must be protected from unauthorized access and misuse. Unlike a password, a biometric trait cannot be changed if compromised, making secure storage a top priority. Subsequently, companies must implement robust data protection measures, ensuring that biometric data are encrypted and only accessible to those with the proper authorization.

Informed consent and user rights are also critical issues. Individuals must be aware of how their biometric data will be used, who will have access, and for how long they will be stored. Transparency in these areas fosters trust and ensures that users retain control over their personal information. In short, ethical considerations must guide the implementation of biometric systems to prevent misuse and protect individual privacy.

Real-world examples highlight the successful use of biometric technologies across various security contexts. In corporate offices, biometric access has become a staple, offering a secure and efficient way to manage employee access. Employees can enter secure areas quickly without the need for badges or PINs, streamlining operations and enhancing security. Airports have also embraced biometric enhancements, using technologies like facial recognition to improve passenger flow and security. In these environments, biometric systems enhance both efficiency and safety, reducing bottlenecks and guaranteeing that only authorized individuals pass through security checkpoints.

As biometric technologies continue to evolve, they promise to further revolutionize identification in security. Their ability to offer accurate and convenient solutions makes them an attractive option for a wide range of applications. However, addressing privacy and ethical concerns is essential to their continued success. By balancing innovation with responsible use, biometric systems can deliver on their promise of enhancing security while respecting individual rights. The future of security identification is bright, with biometrics leading the way.

Data Analytics in Security: From Predictive Policing to Risk Assessment

In the modern landscape of private security, data analytics plays a pivotal role, transforming vast amounts of information into actionable insights. Imagine a city where every datum—from social media posts to traffic patterns—contributes to a comprehensive understanding of crime trends. Predictive modeling allows security firms to anticipate criminal activity by analyzing historical data and identifying patterns. This isn't about predicting crime with crystal ball accuracy; rather, it's about making informed decisions that enhance operational efficiency. For example, if data suggest a rise in thefts during certain times, security resources can be allocated accordingly to deter potential incidents. This strategic use of data helps firms stay one step ahead, mitigating risks before they manifest as real threats.

The benefits of predictive policing techniques extend beyond mere anticipation of crime. By leveraging data analytics, security firms can conduct detailed crime trend analysis, pinpointing hotspots and times of increased activity. This allows for resource allocation optimization, confirming that personnel and equipment are deployed where they're most needed. Such precision not only enhances security but also reduces costs, as resources are utilized more effectively. For policymakers, these insights offer a foundation for crafting targeted interventions and addressing the root causes of crime rather than just its symptoms. The power of data lies in their ability to transform reactive security measures into proactive strategies, ultimately fostering safer communities.

However, the reliance on data-driven security practices is not without its challenges. Ethical and privacy concerns loom large, particularly when it comes to data collection and individual privacy. To address these issues, data anonymization practices are essential. By stripping personal identifiers from datasets, security firms can analyze trends without compromising individual privacy. In this setting, balancing surveillance with privacy rights requires a delicate touch, ensuring that security objectives do not infringe upon civil liberties. Policymakers must navigate this terrain carefully, crafting regulations that protect privacy while enabling effective security measures. This balance is vital for maintaining public trust, a cornerstone of any successful security initiative.

Real-world applications demonstrate the tangible benefits of data analytics in security. In smart cities, data from sensors and cameras are analyzed to optimize everything from traffic flow to emergency response times. These initiatives not only enhance safety but also improve the overall quality of life for residents. In the retail sector, customer behavior analysis helps identify potential security threats, such as shoplifting patterns or suspicious activities. By understanding how individuals move through a store, security teams can deploy resources more effectively, preventing incidents before they occur. These examples highlight the versatility of data analytics, showcasing its potential to revolutionize security across various contexts.

The integration of data analytics into security practices also impacts the roles and responsibilities of security personnel. As data become central to decision-making, the demand for data literacy among security teams increases. Training programs must evolve to equip personnel with the skills needed to interpret and act on data-driven insights. Decision-support systems powered by analytics provide on-ground teams with real-time information, enhancing their ability to respond swiftly and effectively. This shift elevates the role of security personnel from mere enforcers to informed strategists capable of leveraging data to achieve security objectives. The evolution of these roles reflects a broader trend toward intelligence-led security, where data-driven insights inform every aspect of operations.

As we conclude this chapter, it's evident that technology and innovation are reshaping the landscape of private security. From data analytics to drones and robotics, each advancement offers new tools and techniques to enhance safety and efficiency. Yet, with these innovations come new challenges, particularly in the realms of ethics and privacy. As we transition to the next chapter, we'll explore how these technological shifts influence the legal frameworks and ethical considerations that govern private policing, setting the stage for a deeper understanding of the complex interplay between technology and security policy.

Chapter 4:

Collaboration and Integration

With Public Law Enforcement

Imagine a city where the lines between public and private sectors blur, not in a chaotic way but through a strategic partnership aimed at enhancing public safety. Public-private partnerships (PPPs) in security are not a novel concept, yet they represent a rapidly evolving strategy to address the modern challenges of law enforcement. At their core, these partnerships are structured frameworks where public police forces and private security firms collaborate to achieve mutual goals. They share responsibilities, resources, and expertise to create a more comprehensive safety net for communities. This collaborative approach is designed to optimize the strengths of both sectors, ensuring that public safety is maintained efficiently and effectively.

In these partnerships, shared security responsibilities mean that both public and private entities contribute to the safety of a community. The police may focus on law enforcement and legal proceedings, while private firms handle surveillance, crowd control, or specific site security. Collaborative resource allocation is another key component, allowing both parties to pool their resources for maximum impact. For instance, a city might use public funds to support technology upgrades in private security systems, benefiting from the advanced capabilities without bearing the full cost. This synergy not only enhances operational effectiveness but also allows for more strategic deployment of resources, ensuring that both public and private efforts are complementary rather than duplicative.

Benefits & Challenges

The benefits of PPPs extend beyond just operational efficiency. Cost-sharing is a significant advantage, as it guarantees the distribution of expenses associated with implementing advanced security measures. Public agencies strapped for cash can leverage private investments to upgrade security infrastructure while private firms gain access to public resources and networks.

Moreover, these partnerships often provide increased access to advanced technologies that might otherwise be cost-prohibitive. For example, private security firms might utilize cutting-edge surveillance equipment, funded in part by public grants, to monitor critical infrastructure. This access ensures that both public and private entities can use state-of-the-art tools to enhance their security capabilities.

However, forming effective PPPs is not without its challenges. Differing organizational cultures can pose significant obstacles to successful collaboration. Public agencies often operate within a bureaucratic framework, emphasizing procedure and protocol, while private firms may prioritize flexibility and efficiency. These administrative differences can lead to misunderstandings or friction when aligning operational goals. Resistance to information sharing further complicates these partnerships. Public agencies may be hesitant to share sensitive data with private firms due to privacy concerns, while private entities may guard proprietary information. Overcoming these barriers requires building trust and establishing protocols that ensure data are protected while still enabling effective collaboration.

Despite these challenges, there are numerous examples of successful PPPs in security. Citywide surveillance projects are one such example, where public and private entities work together to create an integrated surveillance network. In these projects, private firms may provide the technology and expertise, while public agencies ensure compliance with legal standards and maintain oversight. A notable case is the integration of camera networks into urban centers, which has highly improved crime detection and response times.

Joint emergency response initiatives also highlight the potential of PPPs. In these scenarios, public and private teams coordinate to manage crises, such as natural disasters or large public events. By leveraging the strengths of both sectors, these initiatives ensure a rapid and comprehensive response, minimizing the impact on communities.

Visual Element: PPP Case Study Infographic

Consider a visual element that outlines a successful public-private partnership in security. This infographic could detail a specific case, highlighting the shared responsibilities, resources, and technologies utilized. By exploring such a visual representation, you gain a deeper understanding of how these partnerships function and the tangible benefits they offer to communities.

Communication and Coordination: Overcoming Collaboration Barriers

Communication stands as the backbone of any successful partnership, especially in the realm of public-private security collaborations. Imagine a scenario where public police and private security firms work side by side yet operate in silos due to poor communication. The outcome is predictable: inefficiencies, misaligned objectives, and potentially compromised security.

Effective communication facilitates transparency in operations, confirming that all parties are on the same page. Regular interagency meetings are critical, providing a platform for discussing strategies, sharing insights, and aligning goals. These meetings foster a culture of openness where concerns can be addressed promptly and collaborative solutions can be crafted. By establishing a routine communication cadence, public and private entities can build stronger relationships, enhancing their ability to respond cohesively to security challenges.

Despite its importance, communication between public and private security entities often faces considerable barriers. Differing terminologies and protocols are among the most common obstacles. Public agencies may use language steeped in legal jargon and procedural codes, while private firms might employ industry-specific terms that are foreign to their public counterparts. This disconnect can lead to misunderstandings, where critical information is lost or misinterpreted.

Information silos further compound the problem. When data and insights are not shared freely, each entity operates with an incomplete picture, hindering its ability to make informed decisions. These silos can stem from mistrust, where parties are hesitant to disclose information due to concerns over confidentiality or competitive advantage. Such barriers not only impede effective coordination but also weaken the overall security framework.

To bridge these communication gaps, standardized communication platforms offer a practical solution. By adopting shared tools and systems, public and private entities can streamline their interactions, ensuring that information flows smoothly and securely. These platforms can facilitate real-time communication, enabling quick responses to emerging threats.

Additionally, developing joint communication protocols is paramount. These protocols establish a common language and set of procedures for all parties to follow, reducing the risk of misunderstandings and ensuring that everyone operates according to the same playbook. Training sessions focused on these protocols can further enhance understanding and compliance, equipping personnel with the skills needed to communicate effectively across organizational boundaries.

The impact of improved communication on security outcomes is profound. When public and private entities coordinate effectively, response times in emergencies are much faster. Imagine a critical incident where both sectors are mobilized swiftly, thanks to seamless communication. Such coordination guarantees that resources are deployed efficiently, reducing the needed time to control and mitigate threats. Moreover, improved communication fosters trust between agencies. When entities share information openly and collaborate transparently, they build confidence in each other's capabilities and intentions. This trust is invaluable, as it encourages continued collaboration and reduces the likelihood of conflicts or disputes. Over time, it lays the foundation for a robust partnership that can adapt to changing security landscapes, ensuring that both public and private entities are well-equipped to safeguard their communities.

Effective communication is more than just exchanging information; it's about building a culture of collaboration where all parties are committed to working together toward common goals. By prioritizing transparency, leveraging standardized tools, and fostering trust, public and private security entities can overcome communication barriers and enhance their collective impact. As you consider the role of communication in these partnerships, reflect on how these principles apply to your own interactions and collaborations.

Joint Training Initiatives: Bridging the Gap Between Public and Private Forces

In a world where public and private security forces work together seamlessly, their operations are synchronized as if they were a single entity. This vision is increasingly becoming a reality through joint training initiatives. These programs are designed to break down the barriers between public police and private security firms, fostering a culture of mutual respect and understanding. Cross-training in tactical operations is one of the most effective ways to achieve this. By participating in joint exercises, both forces learn to anticipate each other's moves, creating a cohesive unit that can respond swiftly and effectively to threats. Shared workshops on security technologies further enhance this interoperability, providing a platform for both sectors to explore new tools and methods. These workshops not only introduce participants to cutting-edge technology but also encourage the exchange of ideas, sparking innovation and collaboration.

The success of joint training programs hinges on several key components. Scenario-based exercises are perhaps the most important as they simulate real-life situations and allow participants to practice their skills in a controlled environment. By mimicking the unpredictability of real-world incidents, these scenarios prepare both public and private forces for the unexpected, teaching them to adapt to evolving situations. The inclusion of diverse security expertise is also vital. By bringing together experts from different fields, these programs ensure a well-rounded approach to training. This diversity enriches the learning experience, exposing participants to a wide range of perspectives and strategies.

Despite their benefits, joint training initiatives often face powerful challenges. Logistical constraints can impede the effectiveness of these programs. Coordinating schedules, securing venues, and allocating resources can be complex and time-consuming. These logistical issues require careful planning and flexibility to overcome. Differences in training methodologies further complicate matters. Public police forces may follow rigid, standardized procedures, while private firms often adopt more flexible, client-specific approaches. Bridging these differences requires a willingness to compromise and adapt, ensuring that both sectors can work together without sacrificing their unique strengths.

Real-world examples highlight the impact of effective joint training programs. Multiagency disaster preparedness drills are a prime example. These exercises bring together public and private entities to simulate large-scale emergencies, such as natural disasters or terrorist attacks. By working together in these high-pressure scenarios, both forces develop a shared understanding of each other's capabilities and limitations, improving their ability to coordinate during actual crises.

Joint cybersecurity workshops also demonstrate the value of collaboration. In these sessions, participants from both sectors explore the latest cyber threats and defenses, sharing insights and strategies to protect critical infrastructure. These workshops foster a sense of community and cooperation, strengthening the collective response to cyber threats.

Textual Element: Training Scenario Reflection Exercise

Consider a training scenario reflection exercise where you envision a joint training session between public police and private security forces. Reflect on the dynamics of the session, the challenges faced, and the lessons learned. How did the participants overcome differences in procedures? What strategies were most effective in fostering collaboration? This exercise can provide valuable insights into the intricacies of joint training initiatives and their potential to enhance public safety.

Shared Intelligence Networks: Enhancing Security Through Information Sharing

The landscape of modern security is increasingly defined by the ability to share and analyze information swiftly and accurately. Shared intelligence networks serve as the backbone of public-private security collaborations, facilitating the exchange of crucial data that enhance the effectiveness of both sectors. These networks allow for real-time crime data sharing, which is pivotal in identifying and responding to emerging threats. Imagine a system where public police can instantly share crime reports or suspect descriptions with private security firms, enabling a coordinated response that greatly reduces the time it takes to address a threat. Collaborative threat analysis also benefits from these networks, as both public and private entities can pool their expertise and resources to assess potential risks, ensuring a comprehensive understanding of the security landscape.

The benefits of intelligence sharing in security operations are manifold. Access to shared intelligence empowers security forces to develop proactive crime prevention strategies, moving beyond reactive measures to anticipate and mitigate threats before they materialize. For instance, by analyzing data on past incidents, security teams can identify patterns and implement measures to deter criminal activities. Enhanced situational awareness is another major advantage, allowing security personnel to maintain a real-time overview of unfolding events. This heightened awareness enables quicker decision-making and more effective allocation of resources, ultimately leading to improved security outcomes.

Despite the clear advantages, establishing and maintaining shared intelligence networks is challenging. Data privacy concerns are at the forefront, as the exchange of sensitive information must be conducted with stringent safeguards to protect individual rights. Balancing the need for security with the imperative of privacy requires robust data protection measures and transparent policies that reassure all stakeholders. Technical interoperability issues also pose significant hurdles. Different agencies and organizations may use disparate systems and technologies, complicating efforts to seamlessly integrate and share data. Overcoming these challenges necessitates a commitment to developing standardized protocols and investing in compatible technologies that facilitate smooth data exchange.

Examples of Successful Collaborations

Examples of successful intelligence-sharing initiatives abound, showcasing the potential of these networks to transform security operations. Fusion centers, which integrate data from multiple sources to provide a unified picture of threats, stand as a testament to the power of collaborative information sharing. These centers bring together public and private entities, fostering an environment of cooperation and mutual support. Similarly, cross-border intelligence collaborations have proven effective in addressing transnational threats. By sharing intelligence across national boundaries, countries can coordinate their efforts to combat issues such as terrorism, cybercrime, and trafficking, enhancing global security and stability.

Interactive Element: Intelligence-Sharing Scenario Exercise

Consider engaging in an intelligence-sharing scenario exercise. Envision a situation where a security team must collaborate with local law enforcement and private firms to address a potential threat. Reflect on the steps taken to share information, the challenges faced, and the strategies employed to ensure effective collaboration. This exercise can provide valuable insights into the intricacies of intelligence-sharing networks and their impact on security operations.

The role of shared intelligence networks in public-private security collaborations cannot be overstated. By facilitating the exchange of critical information, these networks enhance the ability of both public and private entities to respond to and prevent threats. While challenges such as data privacy and technical interoperability must be addressed, the benefits of intelligence sharing are undeniable. As security landscapes evolve, the importance of these networks will only grow, underscoring the need for continued investment and innovation in intelligence-sharing initiatives.

Case Studies in Collaboration: Successful Models and Lessons Learned

In exploring successful models of public-private security collaborations, the City of London's Ring of Steel project emerges as a beacon of strategic integration. This initiative, established in response to the IRA bombings in the 1990s, showcases a robust partnership between law enforcement and private security entities. The Ring of Steel employs a comprehensive network of surveillance cameras and roadblocks, monitored collaboratively by both sectors, which ensures that security personnel are not just passive observers but active participants in the city's defense strategy. The project's success lies in its ability to deter threats while maintaining a fluid exchange of information between public and private players. This seamless interaction is underpinned by a shared commitment to safeguarding the city, a testament to the power of unity in addressing complex security challenges.

Across the Atlantic, New York City's Lower Manhattan Security Initiative (LMSI) offers another compelling example. Following the 9/11 attacks, this initiative was launched to bolster security in a high-risk area. It integrates over 3,000 surveillance cameras, license plate readers, and radiation detectors into a centralized command center. This hub serves as a nerve center where both public police forces and private security firms converge, sharing data and resources. The LMSI's strength lies not just in its technological prowess but in its governance structure. Strong leadership ensures that all stakeholders are aligned with the initiative's objectives, fostering an environment where collaboration thrives. By facilitating clear communication channels and establishing a unified command structure, the LMSI exemplifies how effective coordination can enhance security outcomes in even the most challenging environments.

The success of these collaborations can be attributed to several key factors. Strong leadership and governance create a cohesive framework within which diverse entities can operate effectively. In both the Ring of Steel and the LMSI, leadership plays a pivotal role in aligning strategic goals and ensuring accountability. Clear communication channels further underpin these partnerships, enabling swift information exchange and coordinated responses. These channels are not just about the flow of data but also about fostering a culture of trust and mutual respect. When communication is open and transparent, it paves the way for successful teamwork and innovation.

Lessons learned from these case studies highlight the critical importance of stakeholder engagement. Active involvement of all parties, from government agencies to private firms and community representatives, guarantees that diverse perspectives are considered. This inclusivity fosters a sense of ownership and commitment to shared security goals.

Adaptability to evolving threats is another important takeaway. Both initiatives have demonstrated the ability to respond to changing security landscapes, whether through technological upgrades or tactical adjustments. This flexibility is essential in a world where security threats are constantly evolving, which requires dynamic solutions.

The scalability and adaptability of these models offer insights into their potential replication in different contexts. Customization for local needs is paramount; each city or region has its unique security challenges and cultural nuances. By tailoring approaches to fit local circumstances, these models can be effectively transferred and implemented elsewhere. Integration with existing security infrastructures is equally vital, ensuring that new initiatives complement rather than replace established systems. This approach not only enhances efficiency but also builds on existing strengths, creating a more resilient security framework.

In conclusion, the Ring of Steel and the LMSI illustrate the transformative power of public-private partnerships in security. Their success stories underscore the importance of leadership, communication, stakeholder engagement, and adaptability. As cities worldwide grapple with complex security challenges, these models serve as invaluable blueprints for fostering effective collaborations that safeguard communities.

Policy Frameworks for Public-Private Security Integration

Policies play a pivotal role in shaping how the public and private sectors collaborate in security efforts. They provide the scaffolding that supports these partnerships, ensuring that both sectors can work together effectively and efficiently. Regulatory guidelines are a key component, offering a blueprint for collaboration that aligns with legal requirements and societal expectations. These guidelines define the roles and responsibilities of each party, setting clear boundaries and expectations that help prevent conflicts and misunderstandings. By providing a structured framework for cooperation, regulatory guidelines enable public and private entities to focus on their shared goal of enhancing community safety.

Incentives for private sector involvement are another vital element of effective policy frameworks. By offering benefits such as tax breaks or grants, governments can encourage private firms to invest in public safety initiatives. These incentives not only help offset the costs associated with security operations but also foster a sense of shared responsibility. When private firms see tangible benefits from participating in public safety efforts, they are more likely to commit their resources and expertise to these initiatives. This commitment is essential for building strong, sustainable partnerships that can adapt to changing security landscapes.

An effective policy framework must include several key components to facilitate successful integration. Legal and operational standards are fundamental, confirming that all parties adhere to the same rules and procedures. These standards provide a common language for collaboration, making it easier for public and private entities to work together without friction.

Mechanisms for accountability and oversight are equally important, as they ensure that both sectors remain transparent and responsible in their actions. By establishing clear channels for monitoring and evaluation, policy frameworks can help build trust between public and private partners, fostering a culture of openness and cooperation.

Despite their importance, developing and implementing policy frameworks presents significant challenges. One significant obstacle is balancing public interest with private sector goals. Public agencies may prioritize community welfare and safety, while private firms may focus on profitability and efficiency. Therefore, finding a middle ground that satisfies both parties requires careful negotiation and compromise. Facing complex regulatory environments is another challenge, as the patchwork of local, national, and international laws can create confusion and uncertainty. Policymakers must work diligently to harmonize these regulations, ensuring that policy frameworks are clear, coherent, and adaptable to different contexts.

Successful policy frameworks demonstrate how effective collaboration can be achieved. The U.S. National Infrastructure Protection Plan is a prime example, providing a comprehensive strategy for protecting the nation's critical infrastructure through public-private partnerships. This plan outlines a coordinated approach that leverages the strengths of both sectors, emphasizing the importance of shared responsibility and mutual support. In Europe, E.U. directives on public-private collaboration offer another model of success. These directives establish a framework for cooperation that addresses common challenges and promotes the best practices across member states. By fostering a spirit of collaboration and innovation, these policies have paved the way for successful partnerships that enhance regional security and resilience.

As I bring this chapter to a close, the importance of robust policy frameworks in facilitating public-private security integration is unmistakable. These frameworks guide collaborative efforts, align goals, and establish trust, guaranteeing that both sectors can work together to create safer communities. The journey of integrating public and private security efforts is ongoing, shaped by evolving challenges and opportunities, and it is through these policy frameworks that we can confront this complex landscape successfully.

Chapter 5:

Risk Management and Crisis

Preparedness

Imagine standing at the helm of a vast ship, navigating through the unpredictable waters of modern security. The waves represent the myriad risks that threaten to disrupt the course—some visible, others lurking beneath the surface. In the realm of private policing, understanding and managing these risks is paramount. Risk assessment is not merely a task; it is a strategic endeavor that guides security operations and informs decision-making processes. For college students and policymakers, mastering this discipline is essential, as it provides the foundation for robust security strategies that safeguard both private interests and public safety. In this chapter, we will explore the methodologies that underpin effective risk management, equipping you with the tools to identify, evaluate, and communicate potential threats with precision and clarity.

Risk Assessment Methodologies and Techniques

Risk assessment methodologies provide a structured approach to identifying and evaluating potential threats, guiding security professionals in their quest to safeguard assets and operations. Among these methodologies, SWOT analysis stands out as a versatile tool. By examining strengths, weaknesses, opportunities, and threats, security firms can gain a comprehensive understanding of their current position and future prospects. This analysis not only highlights internal capabilities and vulnerabilities but also uncovers external opportunities and threats that may impact security operations. For instance, a security firm operating in a high-crime area might identify its well-trained personnel as a strength while recognizing limited access to advanced technology as a weakness. Opportunities may arise from emerging security technologies, while threats could include rising crime rates or new regulatory challenges. By systematically assessing these factors, firms can develop strategies that leverage their strengths, address weaknesses, capitalize on opportunities, and mitigate threats.

Scenario planning techniques further enhance risk assessment by allowing security professionals to envision and prepare for potential future events. These techniques involve creating detailed narratives of possible scenarios, ranging from minor incidents to major crises. By exploring various outcomes, security teams can develop flexible strategies that adapt to changing circumstances.

Furthermore, scenario planning encourages proactive thinking, helping firms anticipate challenges and devise contingency plans. For example, a security company might create scenarios involving a cyberattack on critical infrastructure, a natural disaster disrupting operations, or a significant change in regulatory requirements. By considering these possibilities, firms can identify potential vulnerabilities and develop comprehensive response plans that enhance resilience and adaptability.

Threat and vulnerability assessments (TVAs) offer another layer of insight, focusing on identifying specific threats and assessing the vulnerabilities that could be exploited. TVAs involve a systematic examination of both physical and digital assets, evaluating their susceptibility to various risks. This process often includes analyzing the likelihood and impact of potential threats, such as unauthorized access to sensitive data or physical breaches of secured areas. By identifying vulnerabilities, firms can implement targeted measures to strengthen their defenses, reducing the likelihood of successful attacks.

TVAs are particularly valuable in today's interconnected world, where threats can emerge from both traditional and cyber domains. Therefore, by integrating TVAs into their risk management strategies, security firms can create a comprehensive defense posture that addresses both current and emerging threats.

Moreover, qualitative and quantitative risk assessment techniques provide different lenses to evaluate security threats, each offering unique insights. Qualitative techniques focus on descriptive analysis, using expert judgment and subjective evaluations to assess risks. These techniques are valuable for understanding complex, multifaceted threats that may not lend themselves to numerical analysis. For example, a qualitative assessment might involve interviews with security personnel to gauge their perceptions of potential threats and vulnerabilities.

In contrast, quantitative techniques rely on numerical data and statistical models to evaluate risks. These techniques allow for precise calculations of risk probabilities and impacts, enabling data-driven decision-making. In this context, risk matrix development is a common quantitative approach, plotting the likelihood of various threats against their potential impact. This visual representation helps prioritize risks, guiding resource allocation and mitigation efforts. Similarly, cost-benefit analysis evaluates the financial implications of security measures, weighing the costs of implementation against the benefits of risk reduction. By employing both qualitative and quantitative techniques, security firms can develop a nuanced understanding of risks, informing strategic decisions and enhancing overall security.

In the ever-evolving landscape of security, continuous risk monitoring is essential. Threats are dynamic and constantly changing in response to technological advancements, geopolitical shifts, and societal trends. To stay ahead, security firms must implement continuous threat monitoring systems that provide real-time insights into emerging risks. These systems leverage advanced technologies, such as artificial intelligence and machine learning, to detect anomalies and predict potential threats. By analyzing vast amounts of data, these systems can identify patterns and trends that may signal impending risks, allowing firms to act swiftly and decisively. Regular risk audits and reviews complement these systems, providing opportunities to reassess vulnerabilities and update risk management strategies. Through ongoing monitoring and assessment, security firms can maintain a proactive stance, anticipating and mitigating threats before they materialize.

On the other hand, effective risk communication and reporting are essential components of risk management, ensuring that stakeholders are informed and engaged. Clear communication of risk information fosters transparency and facilitates collaboration, enabling stakeholders to make informed decisions. Risk communication templates provide standardized formats for conveying risk assessments and highlighting key findings and recommendations. These templates guarantee consistency and clarity, enhancing the credibility of the information presented.

Stakeholder engagement strategies further support risk communication, encouraging dialogue and collaboration between security firms and their clients. By involving stakeholders in the risk assessment process, firms can gain valuable insights and perspectives, enriching their understanding of potential threats and informing the development of tailored risk management strategies. Ultimately, effective risk communication and reporting build trust and confidence, reinforcing the partnership between security firms and their clients.

Interactive Element: Risk Assessment Checklist

To enhance your understanding of risk management, consider creating a personalized risk assessment checklist, which could include key steps such as identifying assets, evaluating vulnerabilities, assessing potential threats, and prioritizing risks. Reflect on how these steps apply to your personal or professional context, considering the unique risks you may face. This exercise will not only deepen your knowledge but also equip you with practical tools to address the complexities of risk management.

Developing Crisis Management Plans: Strategies for Preparedness and Response

You're standing in a room filled with tension as a crisis looms and every decision carries weight. How do you prepare for such moments? A comprehensive crisis management plan is your blueprint for encountering these turbulent waters. It begins with defining clear roles and responsibilities for crisis teams. Each member must understand their specific duties, from communication leaders to logistics coordinators, ensuring that every action is coordinated and purposeful. This clarity minimizes chaos and enhances efficiency, allowing the team to respond swiftly and effectively. Decision-making hierarchies are equally vital, establishing who makes critical decisions and when. This reduces delays and prevents confusion, confirming that the response is both timely and decisive.

Preparing an organization for potential crises involves more than just having a plan on paper. It requires a commitment to regular crisis simulations and drills. These exercises simulate real-life scenarios, testing the organization's readiness and identifying areas for improvement. Through these drills, teams can practice their responses, enhancing their ability to act under pressure.

Resource allocation and management also play a vital role. Organizations must ensure that the necessary resources—whether personnel, equipment, or information—are available and accessible in times of crisis. This involves maintaining an inventory of essential supplies and establishing protocols for rapid deployment. By continuously refining these strategies, organizations build resilience and confidence and stay ready to face the unexpected with poise.

Flexibility and adaptability are the cornerstones of a robust crisis management plan. In the throes of a crisis, conditions can change rapidly, demanding quick adjustments to strategies and actions. Adaptive strategies are essential, allowing organizations to pivot in response to new information or shifting circumstances. This flexibility is supported by the incorporation of real-time data into crisis plans. By leveraging technology to gather and analyze data, organizations can make informed decisions that reflect the current situation. This dynamic approach ensures that responses are not only effective but also relevant, addressing the nuances of each unique crisis. The ability to adapt is what transforms a static plan into a living document capable of guiding organizations through the uncharted territories of crisis.

Consider the financial sector, where corporate crisis management is paramount. Financial institutions face a myriad of potential crises, from cyberattacks to market volatility. Successful crisis management in this sector involves meticulous planning and rapid response. For instance, during a data breach, a bank might activate its crisis team, initiating protocols to secure data and communicate with stakeholders. The plan would include steps for restoring services and protecting customer information, all while maintaining transparency and trust.

In health care, emergency preparedness is equally important. Hospitals must be ready to respond to natural disasters, disease outbreaks, and other emergencies. Effective crisis management plans in health care often include partnerships with local agencies, ensuring that resources and expertise are pooled for maximum impact. These plans prioritize patient safety, continuity of care, and clear communication with the public. By examining these examples, we notice that successful crisis management is not about preventing crises altogether but about being prepared to respond with agility and effectiveness when they occur.

Textual Element: Crisis Management Case Study

Let's delve into a case study of a health care facility that faced a severe influenza outbreak. The hospital's crisis plan included predetermined roles for medical staff, communication protocols for patient and family updates, and resource management strategies to ensure adequate medical supplies. By implementing regular drills, the staff was well-prepared to handle the influx of patients, coordinate with local health departments, and manage public information. This proactive approach minimized disruption and ensured patient care remained a priority. Reflecting on this example, consider how similar strategies might be applied in your own context, reinforcing the importance of preparedness and adaptability in crisis management.

Incident Response Protocols: Managing Security Breaches Effectively

Suppose a bustling retail store suddenly plunges into chaos due to a data breach. The systems falter, customer information is at risk, and the clock is ticking. This scenario underscores the critical importance of having robust incident response protocols in place. These protocols are the backbone of effective breach management, structured to guide security teams through the tumultuous process of identifying, mitigating, and recovering from security incidents.

1. The first stage in any incident response protocol is detection and analysis:

    a. This involves identifying unusual activities or anomalies that may indicate a security breach. Advanced monitoring systems play a pivotal role here, scanning for irregularities in data flow or unauthorized access attempts.

    b. Once a potential breach is detected, the analysis begins. Security teams must swiftly evaluate the nature and scope of the incident, determining whether it is a false alarm or a genuine threat.

2. This evaluation sets the stage for the next critical phases: containment, eradication, and recovery. Containment strategies are designed to limit the breach's impact, isolating affected systems to prevent further damage. This might involve disconnecting compromised devices from the network or implementing temporary safeguards to halt the breach's spread.

3. Following containment, the focus shifts to eradication—removing the threat from the environment. This could mean deleting malicious software, closing security gaps, or enhancing system defenses.

4. Finally, the recovery phase involves restoring normal operations and ensuring all systems are secure and running smoothly.

Incident response teams are the heroes of this process. Comprising specialists with diverse expertise, these teams are tasked with managing incidents from start to finish. Their structure is often hierarchical, with each member assigned specific roles and responsibilities. For example, an incident commander might oversee the entire operation, while technical experts focus on containment and eradication. Communication specialists ensure stakeholders are informed throughout the process, maintaining transparency and fostering trust. This division of labor is vital, as it enables the team to tackle multiple aspects of the incident simultaneously, thereby accelerating response times and minimizing disruptions.

Thorough documentation and reporting are indispensable elements of incident management. Every action taken during a breach must be meticulously recorded, creating a comprehensive log of the incident. This documentation serves several purposes: It provides a detailed account for post-incident analysis, aids in legal compliance, and supports insurance claims if necessary. Incident logging procedures ensure that all relevant information is captured, from the initial detection to the final resolution.

Additionally, post-incident reporting templates offer a standardized format for summarizing the event, highlighting key findings, and outlining lessons learned. These reports are invaluable for future planning, as they help organizations refine their incident response strategies and enhance their overall security posture.

Consider a retail business that successfully faced a major data breach. The company's incident response team acted swiftly upon detecting the breach, isolating affected systems within minutes. By following their established protocols, they contained the threat before it could spread further. The team then worked diligently to eradicate the malicious software, deploying patches and strengthening defenses to prevent future attacks. Throughout the process, they maintained clear communication with both internal stakeholders and affected customers, providing regular updates and reassurance. Thanks to their prompt and coordinated efforts, the business minimized financial losses and preserved customer trust.

In a corporate office, a physical security breach presents a different challenge. Picture an unauthorized individual gaining access to a restricted area. In this case, the response involves immediate containment—securing the area and removing the intruder. Security personnel trained in incident response swiftly coordinate with law enforcement if necessary and document the event in detail. This documentation not only aids in any subsequent investigations but also informs future security enhancements. By analyzing the breach, the organization identifies vulnerabilities in its access control measures and implements improvements, such as upgraded security systems or enhanced employee training. Through these actions, the company fortifies its defenses, reducing the likelihood of future incidents.

These examples illustrate the power of effective incident response protocols. They demonstrate how a well-prepared team, supported by structured processes and thorough documentation, can navigate the complexities of security breaches with confidence and precision. In an age where threats are ever-present, having these protocols in place is not just the best practice; it's a necessity.

Crisis Communication: Maintaining Control in Emergency Situations

Effective communication during a crisis acts like the rudder of a ship, steering the organization through turbulent waters. It's not just about relaying information; it's about stabilizing the situation and guiding the response. A well-crafted communication plan lays the groundwork for clear and concise messaging. This plan should outline who speaks for the organization, ensuring there's a trained spokesperson ready to address the public and media. Identifying these individuals ahead of time is paramount. They should possess not only communication skills but also the ability to remain calm under pressure. They become the organization's voice, providing reassurance and clarity when confusion and chaos threaten to take hold.

Communicating with internal and external stakeholders requires strategic planning. Internally, employees need information that is timely and relevant to their roles. They should understand how the crisis impacts their responsibilities and what steps they should take. In this context, tailored messages are key. For example, frontline staff might receive updates on operational changes while executives are briefed on strategic decisions. Externally, clients and the media require a different approach. Clients need to know how the crisis affects them and what measures are being taken to protect their interests.

Media communication should be handled with care, balancing transparency with the need to protect sensitive information. Social media channels play a pivotal role in this landscape, offering a direct line to the public. However, these platforms also come with risks, as misinformation can spread rapidly. Therefore, organizations must monitor these channels, responding promptly to inaccuracies while reinforcing their messages.

The challenges of crisis communication are numerous:

- Managing misinformation is one of the most daunting tasks, as false or misleading information can escalate a crisis. This requires constant vigilance and quick action to correct inaccuracies.

- Another challenge is balancing transparency with confidentiality. While stakeholders demand openness, certain details must remain confidential to protect privacy or security interests. Striking this balance requires careful judgment and a clear understanding of legal and ethical boundaries.

- Organizations must also be prepared to face scrutiny and tough questions, maintaining their composure and commitment to truthfulness even when under fire.

Real-world examples highlight the power of effective crisis communication. Take, for example, a company entangled in a corporate scandal. The public relations team must act decisively to manage the fallout, issuing statements that acknowledge the issue, outline corrective actions, and express commitment to resolving the matter. By taking control of the narrative, the company can mitigate damage and begin rebuilding trust. In contrast, government agencies dealing with natural disasters face their own set of challenges. Communication strategies in these scenarios focus on providing timely and accurate information to the public, ensuring safety, and coordinating relief efforts. Officials must convey urgency without inciting panic, guiding communities through the crisis with clarity and empathy.

Crisis communication is an art, blending strategy, empathy, and precision. It's about maintaining control in the face of uncertainty and guiding organizations and their stakeholders through the storm. By investing in robust communication plans and training, organizations can confront crises with confidence, minimizing damage and emerging stronger.

Evaluating Crisis Management Outcomes: Case Studies and Lessons

In the aftermath of a crisis, the dust settles as teams regroup and assess the situation. This moment is essential for evaluating crisis management outcomes, a process that is as vital as the response itself. Postcrisis evaluation allows organizations to dissect their performance, uncovering strengths and identifying areas for improvement. It involves a systematic review of the response, examining what worked, what didn't, and why. Often, criteria for evaluating crisis outcomes include the timeliness of the response, the effectiveness of communication, resource management, and the overall impact on operations and stakeholders. Feedback mechanisms, such as debriefing sessions and stakeholder surveys, provide valuable insights, fostering a culture of continuous improvement. These evaluations are not about assigning blame; they are about learning and evolving, ensuring that future responses are more effective and efficient.

Key metrics play a key role in assessing the effectiveness of crisis management efforts:

- One of the most telling indicators is response time—how quickly the organization mobilized its resources and began addressing the crisis. Speed is often vital in minimizing damage and maintaining control.

- Stakeholder satisfaction is another important metric, reflecting how well the organization communicated with and managed the expectations of those affected by the crisis. This includes employees, customers, partners, and the public.

Understanding these metrics helps organizations gauge their performance objectively, providing a benchmark for future improvements. By tracking these indicators over time, organizations can identify trends, adjust their strategies, and enhance their overall preparedness.

Learning from past experiences is invaluable. Real-world cases offer lessons that can shape future strategies, turning challenges into opportunities for growth. Consider the aviation industry, where crisis management is a matter of life and death. Airlines have faced numerous crises, from technical failures to natural disasters. Each incident has provided insights into the effectiveness of existing protocols and the need for innovation. For instance, the response to volcanic ash clouds disrupting flights in Europe highlighted the importance of real-time data and communication. Airlines learned to improve coordination with meteorological agencies and streamline passenger information systems, reducing confusion and enhancing safety. Similarly, natural disaster response efforts offer lessons in resilience and adaptability. Communities hit by hurricanes or earthquakes have demonstrated the value of strong local networks and resource-sharing agreements, enabling faster recovery and rebuilding efforts.

Incorporating these lessons into organizational practices requires deliberate action. Thus, crisis management protocols should be regularly updated to reflect new insights and best practices. This might involve revising communication strategies, enhancing resource allocation plans, or updating technology infrastructure. Integrating lessons into training programs is equally important, ensuring that teams are prepared to apply new knowledge in real-world scenarios. Besides, scenario-based training exercises can simulate past crises, allowing teams to test their responses and refine their skills. By institutionalizing these improvements, organizations create a culture of preparedness and resilience, where learning from the past becomes part of their DNA.

Real-world examples further illustrate the value of postcrisis evaluation. In the aviation sector, after a significant incident involving a technical malfunction, one airline conducted a thorough review of its response. It identified gaps in the communication process and implemented a new system for real-time updates to passengers and staff. This not only improved future crisis management but also boosted customer confidence.

In another case, a city recovering from a major flood used feedback from residents and emergency responders to enhance its disaster preparedness plans. It invested in better infrastructure, improved evacuation routes, and strengthened community engagement initiatives.

These examples underscore the transformative power of learning from experience, turning setbacks into stepping stones for more robust and effective crisis management.

Training for Crisis Preparedness: Building Resilient Security Teams

In the world of private security, the best-laid plans can quickly unravel without the right training. Effective crisis preparedness hinges on a team's ability to respond to unexpected challenges with confidence and agility. Training is not just about learning protocols; it's about instilling reflexes that enable security personnel to act decisively when every second counts. Customized crisis training programs are pivotal in this process. They tailor the learning experience to specific needs and risks faced by different organizations, ensuring that teams are equipped with the relevant skills to address their unique challenges. These tailored programs are complemented by regular drills and simulations, which provide a safe environment to practice and refine responses. By simulating real-life scenarios, teams can test their strategies, identify weaknesses, and build the muscle memory needed to perform under pressure. This practical experience transforms abstract plans into tangible skills, enhancing the overall resilience of security teams.

The components of an effective crisis training program extend beyond the surface. Scenario-based training exercises are at the heart of impactful programs, offering teams the opportunity to engage with realistic challenges in a controlled setting. These exercises mimic the complexity and unpredictability of actual crises, requiring participants to adapt and innovate on the fly. Realistic simulation environments further enhance this experience, immersing teams in situations that closely resemble the conditions they may face in the field. Whether it's a simulated cyberattack on a company's network or a mock evacuation of a high-rise building, these environments push teams to apply their training in practical, high-stakes settings. As teams handle these scenarios, they learn to collaborate, communicate, and make quick decisions, honing the skills that will serve them well in real crises.

Leadership plays a major role in crisis preparedness training. Strong leaders guide and motivate their teams, instilling a sense of purpose and urgency that drives effective responses. Leadership training for crisis situations focuses on developing the skills needed to inspire confidence and maintain composure under pressure. This includes building decision-making skills that enable leaders to assess situations quickly, weigh options, and make informed choices. Leaders must also cultivate the ability to communicate clearly and authoritatively, ensuring their teams understand their directives and act accordingly. By fostering these capabilities, leaders create a culture of readiness and resilience, empowering their teams to rise to the occasion when crises strike. In environments where stakes are high, the presence of trained leaders can mean the difference between chaos and control.

Organizations with exemplary crisis training programs offer valuable lessons in best practices. The military, for instance, is renowned for its rigorous approach to crisis preparedness. Military training emphasizes discipline, adaptability, and teamwork, qualities that are indispensable in high-pressure situations. Soldiers undergo extensive drills and simulations, preparing them for a wide range of scenarios, from combat operations to humanitarian missions. This comprehensive training ensures that military personnel can respond effectively to any crisis, leveraging their skills and experience to achieve mission objectives.

Similarly, the oil and gas industry exemplifies excellence in emergency response training. Given the industry's inherent risks, companies invest heavily in preparing their personnel for potential crises, such as oil spills or equipment failures. Through regular simulations and cross-disciplinary training, employees learn to manage emergencies with precision and efficiency, minimizing impacts on safety and the environment.

As we conclude this chapter, it's clear that crisis preparedness is not just a set of procedures; it's a mindset. Training transforms theory into practice, equipping teams with the skills and confidence to tackle crises with agility and skill. In the next chapter, we will explore the intersection of technology and private security, examining how innovations are reshaping the landscape and offering new tools to enhance safety and efficiency.

Chapter 6:

Professional Development and

Training in Private Security

Picture a scenario where every security professional is equipped not only with the necessary skills but also with a keen understanding of their role in an ever-evolving landscape. This is the vision that drives the design of effective training programs in private security. In a world where threats are as diverse as they are complex, training programs must be comprehensive and tailored to meet the needs of individuals at every level of the security sector.

Overview of Training Programs

The foundation of any robust training program begins with a thorough needs assessment. This involves identifying the specific skills required for different roles within the organization, which ensures that training objectives are aligned with both immediate operational needs and long-term strategic goals. By understanding these requirements, training programs can be crafted to address the unique challenges faced by security personnel, from frontline guards to cybersecurity experts.

Developing clear learning outcomes is another key component of successful training programs. These outcomes serve as benchmarks for both trainers and trainees, providing a clear road map of what needs to be achieved. For instance, a training module focused on incident report writing might outline specific competencies such as attention to detail and accuracy, confirming that participants understand not just what to do but why it matters. By setting clear, measurable goals, training programs can effectively gauge progress and adjust their content to address gaps in knowledge or skills.

Incorporating realistic training scenarios is essential for bridging the gap between theoretical knowledge and practical application. Role-playing exercises and simulations allow trainees to experience real-world situations in a controlled environment, fostering confidence and competence. For example, cybersecurity personnel might engage in simulations that mimic real cyberattacks, enabling them to apply their knowledge in a dynamic and interactive setting. These scenarios help participants develop critical thinking and problem-solving skills, preparing them to respond effectively to challenges they may encounter in the field.

Recognizing that security roles are not one-size-fits-all, training must be customized to address the diverse responsibilities of different positions. Specialized programs for cybersecurity personnel, for instance, emphasize the technical skills needed to protect digital assets, while tactical training for physical security teams focuses on situational awareness and threat detection. This customization guarantees that each participant receives the targeted training necessary to excel in their specific role, enhancing overall team performance and effectiveness.

Engagement is key to successful learning, and training delivery methods should reflect this. Interactive modules, for instance, encourage active participation, enabling trainees to engage with the material in meaningful ways. Incorporating elements of gamification, such as challenges and rewards, can further enhance engagement by making learning both enjoyable and competitive. These methods not only improve retention rates but also foster a culture of continuous improvement and enthusiasm for learning among security personnel.

Innovative training programs set industry standards and push the boundaries of traditional learning methods. Virtual reality (VR) simulations, for example, offer immersive experiences that replicate crisis scenarios in a safe and controlled environment. These simulations provide an unparalleled level of realism, enabling participants to practice decision-making and crisis-management skills without the risks associated with live training exercises. Similarly, online platforms offer continuous learning opportunities, allowing security personnel to access training materials and resources at their convenience. These platforms support self-paced learning, accommodating diverse schedules and commitments of individuals within the security sector.

Interactive Element: Training Program Design Checklist

Consider using a Training Program Design Checklist to organize your efforts. This could include assessing needs, setting learning objectives, choosing delivery methods, and evaluating outcomes. Reflecting on these elements can help you design a training program that meets the unique needs of your organization and ensures participants are well-prepared to handle the demands of their roles.

Certification and Accreditation in Private Security: Standards and Benefits

In the dynamic field of private security, certification and accreditation hold significant weight. They are more than just pieces of paper; they are badges of credibility and professionalism. In an industry where trust is paramount, recognized credentials such as the Certified Protection Professional (CPP) can set apart one security professional from another. Offered by ASIS International, the CPP is a hallmark of expertise, particularly for those in senior security management roles. It reflects a deep understanding of security principles, business practices, and crisis management. The credential is not just a testament to knowledge but an assurance to clients and employers that the individual is equipped to handle complex security challenges.

Accreditation by reputable bodies like ASIS International reinforces this credibility. It ensures that the programs and professionals adhere to industry-wide standards, promoting a culture of excellence and accountability. For security professionals, pursuing such credentials involves meeting stringent requirements. For instance, obtaining the Physical Security Professional (PSP) designation requires not only a solid foundation in physical security but also a commitment to ongoing education. Candidates must fulfill prerequisites such as relevant work experience and a clear understanding of security systems. Once certified, professionals are expected to maintain their credentials through Continuing Education Units (CEUs), ensuring they stay abreast of the latest developments and innovations in the field.

The benefits of certification extend far beyond personal satisfaction. Credentials like the CPP can significantly enhance career prospects and professional development. They open doors to increased job opportunities and pave the way for career advancement, often leading to roles with greater responsibility and higher compensation. Employers recognize certification as a mark of dedication, expertise, and an unwavering commitment to the profession. This recognition not only boosts an individual's confidence but also elevates their standing within the industry. Certified professionals often find themselves in leadership positions where they can influence organizational strategies and mentor the next generation of security leaders.

Consider the story of a security manager who, after obtaining his CPP certification, saw a marked improvement in his career trajectory. Initially working as a mid-level manager in a regional security firm, he decided to pursue the CPP to better equip himself for the challenges of a rapidly changing security landscape. The rigorous preparation for the CPP exam, which covers domains such as investigations, personnel security, and crisis management, broadened his understanding and sharpened his skills. Upon achieving certification, he quickly advanced to a senior management role within his company, overseeing a team of security professionals and developing innovative security solutions for high-profile clients. This leap in responsibility and influence was a direct result of the credibility and recognition that the CPP provided.

Another case is that of a cybersecurity expert who leveraged certification to gain industry recognition. Working in a field where threats are constantly evolving, she pursued specialized certifications to demonstrate her expertise in cybersecurity principles and practices. These credentials not only validated her skills but also positioned her as a thought leader within her organization. Her certification journey became a catalyst for professional growth, leading to opportunities to speak at industry conferences and contribute to influential publications. Her story underscores how certification can serve as a stepping stone to greater visibility and impact in the security field.

For aspiring security professionals, understanding the significance of certification and accreditation is necessary. These credentials are not mere formalities; they are pathways to achieving excellence and making meaningful contributions to the field of private security. By investing in certification, professionals demonstrate their commitment to continuous learning and dedication to upholding the highest standards of security practice. The journey to certification may be rigorous, but the rewards—both personal and professional—are well worth the effort.

Continuous Professional Development: Staying Ahead in a Dynamic Field

In the fast-paced realm of private security, ongoing professional development is not just a choice; it's a necessity. The landscape of security is in constant flux, with emerging threats and new technologies reshaping how security professionals operate. To remain effective, individuals must adopt a mindset of lifelong learning. This approach not only ensures that they stay current with industry changes but also equips them with the skills needed to tackle unprecedented challenges. Whether it's adapting to the latest cybersecurity threats or integrating cutting-edge surveillance technologies, continuous learning is the key to maintaining relevance and competence in a dynamic field.

There are numerous avenues for professional development, catering to a range of learning preferences and schedules. Industry conferences and seminars provide invaluable opportunities for formal learning. These events bring together experts and practitioners, offering insights into the latest trends and best practices. Attending such gatherings not only enhances knowledge but also fosters networking with peers and leaders in the field. Similarly, online courses and webinars have gained popularity, offering flexibility for those who may be geographically dispersed or time-constrained. These digital platforms provide access to a wealth of information, allowing security professionals to learn at their own pace and revisit materials as needed.

Networking is another imperative component of professional growth. Building relationships with industry peers and experts can open doors to new opportunities and collaborations. These connections provide access to diverse perspectives and experiences, enriching one's understanding of the field. Engaging with professional associations and online forums can facilitate this networking process, creating communities where ideas are exchanged and support is offered. By cultivating a robust professional network, individuals can stay informed about industry developments and gain mentorship from experienced leaders.

Mentorship plays a pivotal role in professional development, offering guidance and support throughout one's career. Establishing mentor-mentee relationships can significantly enhance learning and career advancement. A good mentor provides insights drawn from their own experiences, helping mentees address challenges and make informed career decisions.

Mentorship is not a one-way street; reverse mentoring allows experienced professionals to learn from younger or less experienced colleagues, gaining fresh perspectives and new skills. This symbiotic relationship fosters mutual growth and development, benefiting both parties.

Successful professional development initiatives abound in the security industry, demonstrating the value of continuous learning. Many organizations recognize the importance of investing in their employees' growth, offering corporate sponsorship for advanced training programs. These programs provide employees with opportunities to gain specialized skills and knowledge, enhancing their capabilities and career prospects. Industry associations also play a crucial role in organizing workshops and development sessions that address specific needs and challenges within the field. These initiatives showcase the commitment to fostering a culture of learning and development, guaranteeing that professionals are equipped to meet the demands of an ever-evolving industry.

Textual Element: Professional Development Pathways

Consider reflecting on your own professional development journey. What steps have you taken to stay current in your field? Are there specific skills or areas you wish to develop further? Use this reflection to identify growth opportunities and create a plan to pursue them, leveraging available resources and networks.

Leadership Development in Security: Cultivating the Next Generation of Leaders

In the realm of private security, effective leadership is not merely about authority; it's about guiding teams through complex challenges with poise and clarity. The best leaders in this field are those who excel at making decisions under pressure. They possess the ability to remain calm and analytical in high-stakes situations, evaluating risks and benefits before charting a course of action. This skill is critical in environments where time is scarce and consequences are substantial. Alongside decision-making, strong communication and interpersonal skills set successful leaders apart. They articulate their vision clearly, ensuring that all team members understand their roles and the goals they are working toward. This clarity fosters trust and unity, empowering teams to operate efficiently and effectively.

Leadership development programs are pivotal in preparing individuals for these demanding roles. These programs focus on enhancing strategic thinking and equipping future leaders with the tools to anticipate challenges and devise innovative solutions. Ethical leadership and accountability are also core components, as leaders must navigate the delicate balance between operational demands and ethical considerations. By instilling these principles, programs nurture leaders who are not only effective but also principled and capable of making decisions that reflect both organizational goals and ethical standards. Through these structured learning experiences, participants gain insights into the multifaceted nature of leadership, preparing them to tackle the complexities of security management.

Cultivating leadership skills among security personnel involves more than traditional classroom learning. Role-playing exercises provide invaluable opportunities for individuals to step into leadership scenarios, allowing them to practice decision-making and problem-solving in real-time. These exercises simulate the pressures and dynamics of leadership, offering participants a safe space to experiment and learn from their mistakes. Leadership coaching and feedback sessions further support this development, providing personalized guidance and constructive criticism. Coaches help individuals identify strengths and areas for improvement, encouraging a culture of continuous growth and self-reflection. This personalized approach ensures that each participant receives the support they need to develop their unique leadership style.

Consider the story of a security director who rose through the ranks thanks to a comprehensive leadership development program. Initially joining as an entry-level security officer, she quickly demonstrated potential through her proactive approach and keen problem-solving abilities. Enrolled in a leadership program, she honed her strategic thinking and communication skills, learning to navigate complex security challenges with confidence and poise. Her dedication and growth did not go unnoticed, leading to her promotion to a senior leadership role, where she now oversees a team of security professionals. This journey underscores the transformative power of leadership development, illustrating how targeted training can elevate individuals to new heights.

Women in security management often face unique challenges, but leadership programs are helping to break down barriers and promote gender diversity. Take, for example, the experience of a woman who, through targeted leadership initiatives, rose to become a key decision-maker in her organization. Her journey wasn't without obstacles, but the support and training she received enabled her to develop the resilience and confidence needed to thrive in a male-dominated industry. By participating in workshops focused on leadership and empowerment, she gained the skills to advocate for herself and her team, ultimately driving change and enabling an inclusive workplace culture. Her success story highlights the importance of providing tailored support and resources to all aspiring leaders, ensuring that talent and potential are nurtured, regardless of background or gender.

As we consider the future of leadership in private security, it is clear that investing in development programs is vital. These programs cultivate the skills and attributes necessary for effective leadership, ensuring the next generation is ready to navigate an increasingly complex landscape. By focusing on strategic thinking, ethical leadership, and personalized growth, they lay the foundation for leaders who can inspire and guide their teams toward success.

Interdisciplinary Learning: Integrating Diverse Fields for Holistic Security

Interdisciplinary learning in security brings together insights from various fields, creating a richer and more nuanced understanding of the challenges and solutions in the industry. Take the example of the power of integrating psychology into security practices. By understanding human behavior, security professionals can better anticipate potential threats and manage situations more effectively. A deep dive into the nuances of psychological triggers and responses enables security personnel to predict actions and diffuse tensions before they escalate. This knowledge is invaluable in scenarios involving crowd control or hostage negotiations, where reading and influencing human behavior can make all the difference.

Equally important is the application of engineering principles in designing security systems. Engineers bring a systematic approach to problem-solving, confirming that security measures are not only effective but also efficient and reliable. Through the lens of engineering, security systems are crafted with precision, incorporating redundancies and fail-safes to prevent failure. This approach guarantees that security measures remain robust, even under stress. Note that engineers work alongside security experts to design everything from surveillance systems to perimeter defenses, ensuring they meet rigorous standards of performance and safety.

Furthermore, information technology plays a pivotal role in the integration of cybersecurity into broader security strategies. The digital landscape is fraught with vulnerabilities, and IT specialists bring expertise in safeguarding these virtual environments. By incorporating IT knowledge into security training, professionals can ensure that digital assets are as well-protected as physical ones. This integration is vital in an age where cyber threats are as prevalent as physical ones, and the intersection of IT and security becomes a battleground of innovation and vigilance.

Legal studies also complement security training by providing the regulatory knowledge necessary to address the complex legal landscape. A solid understanding of laws and regulations is vital for ensuring compliance and avoiding legal pitfalls. Security professionals armed with legal insights can make informed decisions that uphold security objectives and legal standards. This knowledge is essential in crafting policies and procedures that are not only effective but also legally sound.

Implementing interdisciplinary approaches in training involves collaboration across various fields. Collaborative projects with professionals from different disciplines facilitate an exchange of ideas and perspectives, enriching the learning experience. Security personnel might work alongside psychologists, engineers, and IT experts, each contributing their unique expertise to tackle complex security challenges. This collaboration encourages creativity and innovation, leading to solutions that are both practical and forward-thinking.

Interdisciplinary workshops and seminars provide platforms for this exchange, bringing together experts and learners from diverse fields. These events offer opportunities to explore new concepts and technologies, promoting a culture of continuous learning and adaptation. By engaging with professionals from various backgrounds, security personnel can broaden their understanding and develop a more holistic approach to security. Such interactions not only enhance individual knowledge but also build networks that can be leveraged for future collaboration and problem-solving.

The security industry has seen successful initiatives that integrate multiple disciplines. Joint training programs with law enforcement and IT experts exemplify the power of interdisciplinary collaboration. These programs combine the tactical expertise of law enforcement with the technical acumen of IT professionals, resulting in comprehensive training that addresses both physical and digital security challenges. Participants learn to apply their skills in coordinated efforts, enhancing their ability to respond to complex threats.

Cross-functional teams in corporate security projects further demonstrate the benefits of interdisciplinary learning. By bringing together professionals from various departments, these teams can tackle security challenges from multiple angles, ensuring that solutions are well-rounded and effective. This approach encourages a culture of innovation where diverse perspectives contribute to creative problem-solving. By integrating knowledge from different fields, security practices become more adaptable, resilient, and capable of responding to the evolving landscape of threats.

Evaluating Training Effectiveness: Metrics and Feedback Mechanisms

When it comes to evaluating the effectiveness of training programs in private security, a multi-faceted approach is vital. Quantitative and qualitative measures provide a holistic view of how well training meets the desired outcomes. Participant satisfaction surveys are often the first step in this process, as they gather immediate feedback from trainees about their experiences, capturing their perceptions of the training's relevance, clarity, and engagement. While satisfaction surveys offer valuable insights, they are not sufficient on their own to determine the effectiveness of a program. Performance assessments post-training are equally important. These assessments evaluate whether participants have successfully acquired the skills and knowledge intended by the training. They might include practical exams, simulations, or real-world task evaluations that reflect the challenges faced in daily operations. By combining these quantitative and qualitative tools, organizations can gain a comprehensive understanding of a training program's impact.

Feedback plays a major role in refining and enhancing training programs. Collecting and analyzing participant feedback provides actionable insights that can inform future improvements. In this setting, feedback forms and focus groups are effective methods for gathering detailed opinions and suggestions from participants. These forums encourage honest and open discussions, allowing trainees to express what worked well and what could be improved. Incorporating this feedback into program improvements is essential for maintaining the relevance and effectiveness of training initiatives. By actively listening to participants and making adjustments based on their input, organizations can create a culture of continuous improvement that benefits both trainees and the organization as a whole.

However, measuring training effectiveness is not without its challenges. One common obstacle is balancing quantitative data with qualitative insights. While metrics like test scores and completion rates provide clear data points, they may not capture the nuances of how training impacts behavior and performance. Therefore, it's important to consider both numerical data and personal experiences when evaluating training outcomes. Another challenge is ensuring alignment with organizational goals. Training programs should support the broader objectives of the organization, enhancing the skills and capabilities needed to achieve strategic priorities. Regularly reviewing and aligning training initiatives with these goals ensures that they remain relevant and impactful.

Several organizations stand out for their robust training evaluation processes. One security firm implemented a comprehensive evaluation framework that integrated both quantitative and qualitative data. This framework included regular surveys, performance assessments, and feedback sessions, creating a continuous feedback loop that informed ongoing training improvements. By systematically analyzing training outcomes, the firm could identify trends, address gaps, and reinforce strengths.

Examples of continuous improvement based on training outcomes are abundant within the industry. For instance, a company might notice that trainees struggle with a particular module and, as a result, revise the content or delivery method to enhance understanding. This iterative approach guarantees that training programs evolve to meet the changing needs of the workforce.

Reflecting on these practices, it becomes clear that effective training evaluation is a dynamic process. It requires a commitment to gathering and analyzing diverse data sources, incorporating feedback, and making informed adjustments. By adopting a comprehensive approach to evaluating training effectiveness, organizations can ensure that their programs not only meet the immediate needs of participants but also contribute to the long-term success of the organization.

As we conclude this chapter, we've explored the intricacies of professional development and training within private security. From designing effective programs to evaluating their impact, each aspect plays a pivotal role in preparing security professionals for the challenges they face. As we transition to the next chapter, let's consider how these training principles apply to broader organizational strategies, ensuring that security teams are not only skilled but also aligned with the goals of their organizations.

Chapter 7:

Case Studies and Real-World

Applications

You're standing at the crossroads of tradition and innovation, where the conventional approaches to security meet the dynamic potential of private policing. This is where high-profile security incidents unfold, offering a lens through which we can analyze the role that private firms play in managing crises. These case studies provide a unique opportunity to dissect the strategies employed, assess their effectiveness, and extract valuable lessons that can inform future practices. By examining these real-world applications, you gain insights into how private security not only responds to immediate threats but also adapts to the broader landscape of public safety.

High-Profile Security Incidents: Analyzing Private Security Responses

The 2012 London Summer Olympics stand as a prominent example of how private security firms can both succeed and falter under intense scrutiny. Tasked with securing one of the world's most significant sporting events, the private security company G4S faced substantial challenges. Initially contracted to provide a robust layer of security, G4S struggled to deliver the promised number of trained personnel. This shortfall was so severe that the U.K. military had to deploy 3,500 soldiers to fill the gap. The incident highlighted the risks of overreliance on a single private entity for large-scale security operations, raising questions about oversight and accountability.

Despite these challenges, private security still played a crucial role in managing the event, utilizing advanced surveillance technologies and coordination strategies to help maintain safety and order. The experience underscored the complexity of integrating private security into public events, emphasizing the necessity of comprehensive planning and contingency measures.

In contrast, the role of private security during the 2020 U.S. Capitol breach presented a different set of dynamics. While the primary responsibility for the Capitol's security fell on public law enforcement, private security companies were involved in various capacities, supporting the protection of nearby federal buildings and private entities. The breach exposed vulnerabilities in coordination and communication between security forces, highlighting the need for seamless integration and information sharing. Private security firms, accustomed to safeguarding corporate environments, faced the challenge of adapting their strategies to an unprecedented political crisis. Their involvement demonstrated the importance of flexibility and rapid response capabilities as private security personnel assisted in securing perimeters and managing access control in the aftermath of the breach. This incident served as a stark reminder of the evolving nature of security threats and the importance of preparedness across all sectors.

The strategies employed by private security during these incidents reveal a common emphasis on rapid response and technological integration. Rapid response teams, trained to handle emergencies, were deployed to mitigate immediate threats and support law enforcement efforts. These teams played a key role in quickly neutralizing risks, demonstrating the importance of having well-prepared personnel ready to act at a moment's notice.

Additionally, the utilization of advanced surveillance technology provided real-time data to guide decision-making processes. For instance, the deployment of cameras and monitoring systems allowed security personnel to track movements, identify potential threats, and coordinated responses effectively. These technologies not only enhanced situational awareness but also facilitate communication between private and public security forces.

However, the effectiveness of private security responses is not without its challenges. While successful deterrence of potential threats is a significant achievement, crowd management remains a persistent issue. Large gatherings, whether at sporting events or political demonstrations, require meticulous planning and execution to ensure safety. The ability to manage crowds effectively depends on clear communication, well-trained personnel, and adaptable strategies. The experiences of the London Olympics and the Capitol breach highlight the importance of these elements as private security firms navigate the complexities of large-scale operations.

The lessons learned from these incidents offer valuable insights into improving security protocols and strategies. One of the key takeaways is the critical importance of real-time communication with public law enforcement. Seamless information sharing enhances coordination and ensures that all parties are operating with the same understanding of the situation. Additionally, robust contingency planning is essential to address unforeseen challenges that may arise during operations. By developing comprehensive backup plans and conducting regular drills, security firms can better prepare for a range of scenarios, minimizing the impact of disruptions.

Interactive Element: Reflection Exercise

Reflect on the role of private security in high-profile incidents. Consider how the strategies employed could be adapted to other contexts, such as corporate or community settings. What lessons can be applied to improve coordination and response in future situations? Use this exercise to explore the broader implications of private security's involvement in public safety.

Private Security in Large-Scale Events: Planning and Execution

Imagine the bustling energy of a major international event, where thousands gather, each with their own expectations and excitement. Behind the scenes, a complex web of planning unfolds, orchestrated to ensure safety and security for all. Private security at large-scale events involves meticulous planning, beginning with comprehensive risk assessment and threat analysis. These initial steps are essential; they allow security teams to identify potential vulnerabilities and anticipate challenges specific to the event's nature and location. By collaborating closely with event organizers and stakeholders, private security firms can tailor their strategies to align with the unique dynamics of each gathering. This integration confirms that security measures are both effective and minimally intrusive, preserving the experience for attendees while maintaining a secure environment.

As the event day arrives, the execution of the security plan springs into action:

- Crowd control measures are paramount, requiring a blend of physical presence and strategic barriers to manage the flow of people effectively.

- Access restrictions are carefully implemented, using both human resources and technology to monitor entry and exit points.

- Mobile command units play a pivotal role in this phase, acting as nerve centers that coordinate the myriad aspects of security operations. These units facilitate real-time communication and decision-making, enabling security personnel to respond swiftly to any incidents or changes in the event's dynamics. The presence of a mobile command unit ensures that all security efforts are unified, enhancing the ability to maintain oversight and control.

However, managing security at large-scale events is demanding. One of the most significant hurdles is handling the sheer volume of attendees. The density of crowds requires precise coordination to prevent bottlenecks and ensure safe movement throughout the venue. Furthermore, seamless communication across security teams is essential to address any issues that arise. This requires robust infrastructure and protocols to ensure all personnel are informed and aligned in their objectives. Overcoming these challenges involves constant vigilance and adaptability, as security teams must be prepared to adjust their strategies in response to real-time developments.

Successful security operations at large-scale events can be seen in examples like the Super Bowl, where private security plays a key role in safeguarding one of the most watched sporting events globally. The planning and execution involved in securing the Super Bowl are extensive, involving coordination with federal, state, and local agencies to develop a cohesive security strategy. Private security firms contribute their expertise in crowd management and advanced surveillance, ensuring that the event proceeds smoothly.

Similarly, international music festivals present unique security challenges, with diverse crowds and expansive venues. Private security firms adapt their approaches to these settings, employing a combination of physical security and technology to monitor and protect attendees, creating an environment where music and safety coexist harmoniously.

The ability to execute successful security operations at large-scale events hinges on the integration of strategic planning, advanced technology, and skilled personnel. By understanding the complexities involved and learning from past experiences, private security firms continue to evolve their practices, ensuring they are well-equipped to meet the demands of any significant gathering. This evolution reflects a broader trend in the security industry, where adaptability and innovation are key to safeguarding the diverse and ever-changing landscapes of large-scale events.

Corporate Security Strategies: Protecting Assets and Information

In the bustling world of corporate security, safeguarding assets is a critical task that requires a strategic blend of technology and human oversight. Picture a corporate headquarters, where access control systems are meticulously designed to manage the flow of personnel and protect sensitive areas. These systems, often employing biometric scanners and key card access, serve as the first line of defense against unauthorized entry. By ensuring that only authorized individuals gain access to specific areas, companies effectively minimize the risk of physical breaches.

The strategic placement of surveillance cameras further enhances this protective layer, allowing security teams to monitor high-risk zones such as server rooms and executive offices. This vigilant watch not only deters potential intruders but also assists in real-time threat detection, enabling swift responses to any suspicious activities. Surveillance footage serves as a valuable tool for investigating incidents, providing irrefutable evidence that supports security personnel in maintaining a secure environment.

While physical security remains vital, the digital realm presents its own set of challenges. In today's interconnected world, cybersecurity has emerged as an indispensable component of corporate security strategies. Protecting digital information is paramount, as data breaches can lead to significant financial losses and reputational damage. This is where data encryption and secure communication protocols come into play. By encrypting sensitive information, companies ensure that even if data are intercepted, they remain unintelligible to unauthorized users.

Secure communication protocols, such as virtual private networks (VPNs), provide an added layer of protection for remote connections, safeguarding data transmitted over potentially insecure networks. In addition, network monitoring tools are employed to detect any signs of intrusion, enabling security teams to respond promptly to potential threats. These measures collectively create a robust cybersecurity framework that complements physical security efforts, ensuring a holistic approach to asset protection.

Maintaining effective corporate security, however, is difficult. Insider threats pose a significant risk, as employees with access to sensitive information may inadvertently or maliciously compromise security. To address this issue, companies implement comprehensive training programs that educate employees about security protocols and the importance of vigilance. These programs emphasize the role of each individual in maintaining security, which promotes a culture of awareness and responsibility. As cyber threats continue to evolve, companies must remain agile in their defense strategies. This involves staying abreast of emerging threats and continuously updating security measures to counter new tactics employed by cybercriminals. By investing in advanced threat detection systems and regularly reviewing security protocols, companies can effectively mitigate these risks and maintain a secure environment.

Innovative practices in corporate security are evident across various industries. In the financial sector, for instance, institutions have enhanced security measures to protect against both physical and digital threats. By integrating advanced biometric systems and employing dedicated cybersecurity teams, these institutions safeguard sensitive financial data and ensure secure transactions. In the technology sector, companies prioritize the protection of intellectual property, investing in cutting-edge security technologies to prevent unauthorized access and data leaks. These firms often employ a combination of physical security, such as restricted access to research and development areas, and digital security, including sophisticated encryption and intrusion detection systems. These initiatives not only protect valuable assets but also demonstrate a commitment to security that builds trust with clients and stakeholders.

Corporate security is a dynamic field that requires constant adaptation to new challenges. The integration of advanced technologies, combined with a proactive approach to insider threats and evolving cyber risks, enables companies to protect their assets effectively. As the landscape of corporate security continues to evolve, the lessons learned from innovative practices across industries will inform future strategies, guaranteeing that companies remain vigilant and resilient in the face of ever-changing security threats.

Community-Based Private Security: Engaging Local Stakeholders

Consider a neighborhood where residents and security personnel work side by side, fostering a sense of community that extends beyond simple protection. This is the essence of community-based private security, where firms actively engage with local communities to enhance safety. Building trust with community members is a fundamental aspect of this approach. Security personnel take the time to interact with residents, attend local meetings, and participate in community events. These interactions help demystify security's role in the neighborhood, breaking down barriers and fostering a sense of mutual respect and collaboration. Trust is not built overnight, but through consistent presence and engagement, security personnel become seen as part of the community rather than outsiders.

Collaborative problem-solving with local stakeholders further strengthens this bond. Security firms work closely with community leaders, local businesses, and residents to identify and address specific safety concerns. This collaborative approach ensures that security measures are tailored to the unique community needs rather than imposing a one-size-fits-all solution. By involving community members in the decision-making process, security initiatives become more effective and well-received. Neighborhood watch programs are a prime example of this collaboration as they empower residents to take an active role in their own safety, with security firms providing support, training, and resources. Through these programs, communities become more resilient, cultivating an environment where safety is a shared responsibility.

The role of private security in supporting community initiatives extends beyond traditional patrols. Security firms often provide additional support for local events, ensuring that gatherings are safe and enjoyable for all attendees. Whether it's a street fair, festival, or farmers market, having security personnel on hand provides peace of mind for organizers and participants alike. Their presence not only deters potential troublemakers but also ensures a swift response to any incidents, allowing the event to proceed smoothly. These efforts to address specific community safety concerns demonstrate a commitment to the well-being of the neighborhood, reinforcing the positive impact of security involvement.

Community-based security initiatives have a profound impact on public perception, influencing trust and cooperation within the community. Improved relationships with local law enforcement are a common outcome, as security firms often act as a bridge between the police and the community. By fostering open lines of communication and collaboration, security personnel help address misunderstandings and build trust between residents and law enforcement officers.

Positive feedback from the community serves as a testament to the effectiveness of these initiatives. Residents often express appreciation for the enhanced sense of security and the proactive approach to addressing their concerns. This feedback not only boosts morale among security personnel but also encourages continued investment in community-based security strategies.

Successful community-based security programs can be found in various urban neighborhoods, where community patrols have made a significant difference in reducing crime and enhancing safety. In these areas, security personnel work closely with residents to monitor the streets, share information, and respond to potential threats. Their presence is not only a crime deterrent but also a source of reassurance for residents. Partnerships with local businesses further enhance these efforts, as business owners collaborate with security firms to implement measures that protect both their establishments and the surrounding community. For example, security firms may assist in installing surveillance cameras or provide training for employees on how to handle security situations.

These partnerships contribute to a safer and more vibrant community where businesses thrive and residents feel secure.

Community-based private security exemplifies the power of collaboration and engagement in creating safer neighborhoods. By building trust, fostering cooperation, and addressing specific safety concerns, security firms play a pivotal role in enhancing community safety. These initiatives not only improve public perception but also demonstrate the potential of private security to contribute positively to the communities they serve.

Innovations in Retail Security: Preventing Theft and Loss

In the bustling world of retail, the challenge of preventing theft and minimizing losses looms large. Retailers are constantly innovating to protect their inventory and maintain profitability. One of the transformative technologies in this arena is Radio Frequency Identification (RFID). RFID tags, unlike traditional barcodes, allow for instant tracking of items within a store. These tags communicate with electronic readers, providing real-time data on inventory levels and movements. This technology not only streamlines inventory management but also acts as a theft deterrent. When an item with an RFID tag passes through sensors at store exits, alarms can trigger, alerting staff to potential shoplifting. This technology integration enhances visibility over assets, enabling retailers to manage stock more effectively and reduce shrinkage.

Another cutting-edge advancement is the use of AI-based surveillance systems, which employ machine learning algorithms to analyze video feeds and detect suspicious behavior. For instance, if a person lingers too long in a high-theft area or exhibits erratic movements, the system can alert security personnel to investigate further. This proactive approach allows for quicker responses to potential threats and reduces reliance on human observation alone. The implementation of AI in surveillance not only improves the accuracy of threat detection but also optimizes the allocation of security resources, allowing staff to focus on more complex tasks that require human judgment.

Private security plays a pivotal role in enhancing retail operations by supporting these technological measures with trained personnel. In this context, loss prevention training is a key component, equipping retail staff with the skills to identify and prevent theft proactively. Employees learn to recognize behavioral cues and employ de-escalation techniques, creating a safer shopping environment for customers and staff alike. Furthermore, the integration of security systems with store operations ensures that all components work harmoniously. Security teams collaborate closely with store management to align security protocols with business objectives, guaranteeing that security measures do not disrupt the shopping experience. This collaboration is vital for maintaining a balance between effective security and customer satisfaction.

Despite these advancements, retail security teams face several challenges. Organized retail crime remains a significant issue, with groups targeting high-value items for resale. Tackling this requires a coordinated approach involving not only in-store measures but also intelligence sharing with other retailers and law enforcement. Another challenge is balancing security measures with customer experience. Overzealous security can deter customers and harm a store's reputation. Therefore, it is crucial to implement measures that are effective yet unobtrusive, creating an environment that feels both secure and welcoming.

In practice, innovative security measures have led to considerable reductions in theft across various retail environments. Consider a major department store chain that overhauled its security operations by implementing RFID technology and AI-based surveillance. This comprehensive approach allowed the store to monitor inventory in real-time, quickly identify discrepancies, and respond to theft attempts efficiently. The result was a marked decrease in shrinkage and improved inventory accuracy, which in turn boosted profitability and customer satisfaction. Similarly, the introduction of facial recognition technology in high-risk retail environments, such as electronics stores, has proven effective in deterring repeat offenders and enhancing overall security. These systems, while raising privacy concerns, are designed to comply with data protection regulations, ensuring that customer rights are respected while prioritizing safety.

Visual Element: Infographic on Retail Security Technology

Visualize the integration of retail security technologies with an infographic showcasing the flow of RFID and AI-based surveillance systems. Highlight how these technologies interact with loss prevention strategies to create a seamless security network within a retail environment. This visual representation can help clarify the complex interplay between technology and personnel in maintaining a secure shopping experience.

Lessons From International Case Studies: Adapting Strategies for Success

As you explore the vast landscape of international private security operations, the diversity of geographic and cultural contexts offers rich lessons. In high-risk regions, private security firms face unique challenges that require tailored strategies. For example, in places like the Middle East and parts of Africa, geopolitical instability demands an agile approach. Private security firms must navigate complex security environments where threats can escalate rapidly. Here, strategies often include fortified compounds, advanced monitoring systems, and specialized training in conflict management. These measures not only protect assets but also ensure the safety of personnel operating in volatile areas.

Cultural sensitivity plays a crucial role in the success of these security strategies. In many regions, understanding local customs and societal norms is as important as any technical security measure. A private security firm in Asia, for example, might need to adapt its protocols to align with regional practices, such as the importance of community relationships and respect for local traditions. This cultural awareness helps gain the trust of local communities, which can be vital for effective operations. Leveraging local expertise is another advantage. By employing local staff who understand the nuances of their environment, firms can enhance their operational effectiveness and adaptability.

Navigating the labyrinth of regulatory frameworks presents a notable challenge for international security firms. Each country has its own set of laws and regulations governing private security operations, from licensing requirements to permissible activities. For instance, what is legally permissible in one country might be restricted in another. This complexity requires firms to invest in comprehensive legal expertise to ensure compliance and avoid potential liabilities. Language and communication barriers further complicate operations. In multilingual regions, miscommunication can lead to operational mishaps. Effective communication strategies, including multilingual training programs and the use of translation technology, are essential to overcoming these barriers.

Adapting successful strategies across borders involves more than just replication; it requires customization to local needs. A strategy that works in South America might not translate directly to Southeast Asia without adjustments for cultural and legal differences. Cross-cultural training for security personnel is instrumental in this adaptation process. By equipping staff with an understanding of regional dynamics and potential cultural sensitivities, firms can ensure smoother operations and greater acceptance by local communities. This training goes beyond language skills, encompassing cultural awareness and conflict resolution techniques tailored to the specific region.

The lessons gleaned from these international case studies highlight the importance of flexibility and cultural intelligence in private security operations. By analyzing successful strategies and adapting them to fit local contexts, security firms can enhance their effectiveness and reputation. The ability to operate successfully across different regions showcases the potential of private security to contribute to global safety and stability, offering a model of adaptability and resilience that can inspire future security innovations.

As we transition from these global perspectives, consider how these strategies can be applied closer to home, addressing the unique challenges and opportunities within domestic contexts. The next chapter will delve into the future directions of private security, exploring how emerging technologies and shifting societal needs will shape the security landscape in the years to come.

Chapter 8:

Future Directions and Policy

Recommendations

In a rapidly changing world, private security stands at the forefront of innovation and adaptation. The landscape is shifting, driven by powerful trends that redefine how security is approached and executed. As college students and policymakers, you are in a unique position to witness and influence these transformations. You may find yourself wondering how artificial intelligence, cybersecurity, and smart city technologies are reshaping the field. The answer lies in the integration of these technologies and the new perspectives they bring to traditional security paradigms.

Harnessing the Potential of Technology

Artificial intelligence and machine learning are not just buzzwords; they are revolutionizing how security is managed and maintained. By analyzing vast amounts of data, AI can predict potential threats before they manifest, offering a proactive approach to crime prevention. This shift toward predictive policing harnesses the power of data to make informed decisions, although it is not without its challenges. Concerns about bias and privacy loom large, as algorithms may inadvertently reinforce existing prejudices found in historical crime data. Yet, the potential of AI to enhance public safety cannot be ignored, as it offers the potential for more efficient and targeted interventions.

The increasing focus on cybersecurity and data protection reflects the digital age's demands. As more aspects of our lives and infrastructure become interconnected, the vulnerabilities multiply. Cybersecurity is no longer just an IT issue; it is a critical component of comprehensive security strategies. The integration of physical and digital security systems creates a holistic approach that addresses threats from all angles. This cyber-physical synergy promotes a robust defense against a spectrum of risks, ensuring that both tangible and intangible assets are safeguarded. This convergence requires a workforce skilled in both realms, which necessitates significant investment in training and development.

Smart city technologies are transforming urban environments, embedding intelligence into the very fabric of our communities. Sensors, cameras, and connected devices work in unison to create a responsive and adaptive security network. These technologies offer real-time insights into urban dynamics, allowing for swift responses to incidents and better resource allocation. However, the adoption of these technologies requires careful consideration of privacy implications, as the line between surveillance and intrusion can easily blur. Policymakers must navigate these waters with sensitivity, ensuring that the benefits of smart technologies do not come at the expense of individual freedoms.

These emerging trends present both challenges and opportunities. The adoption of advanced technologies demands careful management to avoid potential pitfalls. Resistance to change and the complexity of integration can hinder progress, requiring leadership that is both visionary and pragmatic. Yet, these trends also offer fertile ground for innovation and growth. Companies that embrace these changes are not only enhancing their security operations but are also setting new standards for the industry. For example, firms utilizing AI in predictive policing have shown remarkable improvements in crime prevention, yet they must remain vigilant against the risks of bias and misuse.

Visual Element: Predictive Policing Infographic

Consider a visual representation of predictive policing, illustrating how data flow from collection to analysis to action. This infographic could highlight the steps involved and the potential impact on community safety while acknowledging ethical concerns.

Organizations at the forefront of these trends are not just adapting; they are leading. They demonstrate the potential of technology to revolutionize security practices, offering models that others can emulate. As you explore these developments, consider the implications for your own work and studies. The future of security is being shaped now, and you have a role to play in ensuring it is both innovative and inclusive.

Policy Recommendations for Ethical and Effective Private Policing

In the realm of private policing, crafting policies that ensure ethical operations and effective outcomes is a priority. Clear ethical guidelines serve as the foundation for these efforts, confirming that private security firms operate with integrity and respect for the communities they serve. Establishing compliance measures is essential to enforce these guidelines consistently, which not only builds trust but also enhances the legitimacy of private policing in the public eye. When security practices are transparent and accountability is prioritized, the entire industry benefits from increased public confidence. Transparency, after all, is not just about openness but a commitment to ethical standards that resonate with both the public and private sectors.

Government and industry collaboration is necessary in driving policy innovation. By working together, these entities can create a regulatory environment that encourages best practices while allowing flexibility for innovation. Government-industry partnerships are instrumental in developing policies that reflect the realities of the security landscape, addressing both current challenges and future needs. Trade associations play a pivotal role in this process by setting standards that guide firms in maintaining high ethical and operational benchmarks. These associations act as mediators, facilitating dialogue between public entities and private firms to guarantee that policies are both effective and equitable.

Identifying areas for policy intervention and reform is a major step in advancing private policing. Regulatory frameworks must evolve to keep pace with technological advances, such as the deployment of drones and the integration of cybersecurity measures. These technologies offer new capabilities but also present unique challenges that require thoughtful regulation to prevent misuse and protect privacy.

Furthermore, emphasizing workforce diversity and inclusion within private security is vital. Diverse teams are not only more reflective of the communities they serve but also bring varied perspectives that enhance problem-solving and innovation. By addressing these issues through policy reform, the industry can foster a more inclusive and effective security environment.

Moreover, innovative policy initiatives serve as blueprints for future success. Legislative efforts to regulate drone use in security have paved the way for safe and efficient operations, balancing the benefits of aerial surveillance with privacy concerns. These efforts underscore the importance of crafting legislation that adapts to new technologies while safeguarding civil liberties. Policies promoting data privacy in surveillance practices are equally important, as they protect individuals' rights while allowing for effective security measures. Such initiatives demonstrate that with careful planning and execution, policies can enhance both security and privacy, setting a precedent for responsible governance in private policing.

Textual Element: Reflection on Ethical Policies

How might these policy recommendations apply to your local community or area of interest? Reflect on which ethical guidelines and compliance measures could be implemented to improve transparency and accountability. Think about the potential challenges and benefits of government-industry partnerships in shaping these policies.

Through strategic policy development, private policing can address the complex landscape of modern security needs while upholding ethical standards. As we explore these recommendations, it becomes clear that the future of private policing lies in its ability to adapt and innovate responsibly. By fostering collaboration between government and industry while addressing key areas for reform, we can ensure that private security remains a trusted and effective component of public safety.

Rethinking Public Safety: Proposals for New Policing Models

As we consider the future of public safety, it's clear that traditional policing models must evolve to meet the needs of a diverse and changing society. Community-centered security models offer a promising path forward. They prioritize the involvement of local residents in shaping security strategies, ensuring that the voices of those most affected by crime and safety concerns are heard and respected. By empowering communities to take an active role in their own security, these models foster a sense of ownership and accountability. This approach not only enhances trust between residents and security providers but also leverages local knowledge to address specific safety issues effectively.

Decentralized security networks further challenge conventional policing by distributing authority and responsibility across various actors, including private security firms, community organizations, and local governments. This model recognizes that public safety is a shared responsibility, requiring collaboration among all stakeholders. By utilizing decentralized networks, communities can respond more flexibly to emerging threats and adapt quickly to changing circumstances. This flexibility is essential in an era where security challenges are increasingly complex and unpredictable. However, implementing such a model requires careful coordination and clear communication to ensure that all parties work toward common goals without duplicating efforts or creating gaps in coverage.

Private security plays a vital role in these new policing models, integrating seamlessly with public initiatives to provide a holistic approach to safety. Joint public-private safety initiatives enable the pooling of resources and expertise, maximizing the strengths of both sectors. By working together, public and private entities can develop comprehensive strategies that address a wide range of safety concerns, from preventing crime to managing emergencies. Technology is a key enabler of this integration, offering tools that facilitate coordination and enhance situational awareness. For example, shared communication platforms and data analytics systems allow for real-time information sharing, enabling rapid and informed decision-making.

The benefits of alternative policing models are significant. Increased community engagement leads to higher levels of trust and cooperation, essential components of effective public safety. When residents feel actively involved in their own security, they are more likely to support and collaborate with security providers. This engagement also encourages transparency and accountability, as community members hold security actors responsible for their actions. However, these models are rigorous. Coordinating multiple stakeholders with different priorities and resources can be complex and time-consuming. It requires a commitment to ongoing dialogue and compromise to develop and maintain effective partnerships.

Examples of successful alternative models abound. In urban areas, community policing initiatives have transformed neighborhoods by fostering strong relationships between police and residents. These initiatives often involve regular community meetings, joint problem-solving efforts, and the use of technology to enhance communication and transparency. In rural regions, technologically driven safety solutions have proven effective in addressing unique challenges posed by geographic isolation and limited resources. Innovations such as drones for surveillance and mobile apps for reporting incidents enable efficient monitoring and response, even in remote areas. These examples illustrate the potential of reimagined policing models to enhance public safety and community well-being.

Balancing Efficiency, Fairness, and Justice in Private Security

In the realm of private security, the pursuit of efficiency, fairness, and justice is not just an idealistic goal but a practical necessity. Balancing these elements ensures that security services are accessible to all, regardless of socioeconomic status. When security becomes a privilege rather than a right, it undermines the very fabric of community trust and cohesion. Ensuring equitable access means that security resources are distributed based on need rather than financial capability, allowing underserved communities to benefit from protection and peace of mind. This equitable approach can transform how security is perceived, shifting it from a service for the few to a communal asset that enhances the overall quality of life.

Cost-effectiveness remains a critical factor for private security organizations, yet it must not overshadow ethical considerations. The temptation to cut corners for financial gain can lead to compromised standards and practices that harm both the industry and those it serves. Balancing these factors requires a commitment to ethical integrity, where cost savings do not come at the expense of fairness or justice. Implementing equity-focused training programs is one strategy to achieve this balance. By educating personnel on the importance of diversity, inclusion, and cultural competency, security firms can foster environments where all clients are treated with respect and dignity, regardless of background or circumstance.

Transparent accountability systems are another tool for aligning operational goals with ethical standards. These systems provide clear metrics for evaluating performance, ensuring that both successes and shortcomings are visible and addressed. This transparency builds trust with clients and the public, demonstrating a commitment to accountability and continuous improvement. Companies that have successfully implemented such systems often see increased client satisfaction and a stronger reputation in the industry. For instance, organizations that prioritize justice-oriented policies in corporate environments often report higher employee morale and engagement, as personnel feel part of a mission that values ethical conduct as much as operational success.

In addition, leadership plays a pivotal role in promoting fairness and justice within private security. Leaders set the tone for organizational culture, influencing how values are prioritized and enacted. A leadership commitment to diversity and inclusion can drive meaningful change, creating workplaces where diverse perspectives are not only welcomed but actively sought out. This commitment extends beyond hiring practices to encompass all aspects of operations, from decision-making processes to client interactions. Leaders who advocate for ethical decision-making empower their teams to navigate complex situations with integrity and thoughtfulness, ensuring that moral considerations are always part of the equation.

Case studies provide valuable insights into how these principles can be effectively applied. In diverse communities, equitable security practices have been achieved through collaborative efforts that involve local stakeholders in the design and implementation of security strategies. These efforts often result in tailored solutions that address specific community needs while fostering trust and cooperation. In corporate settings, justice-oriented policies have been instrumental in creating inclusive environments where fairness guides both internal and external practices. Such policies not only enhance organizational reputation but also contribute to a more cohesive and motivated workforce, as employees recognize the commitment to ethical and equitable treatment.

The pursuit of efficiency, fairness, and justice in private security is a dynamic process that requires ongoing reflection and adaptation. By embracing these principles, security organizations can fulfill their responsibilities in a way that respects the dignity and rights of all individuals. As you consider the role of private security in your own work or studies, reflect on how these elements can be integrated into your approach, ensuring that the pursuit of safety never comes at the cost of fairness or justice.

Engaging Stakeholders in Security Policy Development

When considering the landscape of private security policy development, the inclusion of diverse stakeholders emerges as a cornerstone for crafting effective and equitable policies. Engaging various voices in the policymaking process guarantees that the resulting frameworks are not only comprehensive but also reflective of the diverse needs and perspectives present in society. This inclusive approach enhances the legitimacy and acceptance of policies, as stakeholders feel a sense of ownership and participation. In practice, inclusive policymaking processes lead to more sustainable and impactful outcomes by drawing on a wealth of experiences and insights. The process of building consensus among stakeholders, though challenging, promotes a collaborative environment where diverse interests can be aligned toward common goals.

Key stakeholders in private security policy development include community groups, civil society organizations, industry leaders, and government agencies. Each brings unique perspectives and priorities to the table. Community groups often advocate for policies that prioritize public safety while safeguarding civil liberties. They emphasize the importance of transparency and accountability, ensuring that security measures do not infringe on individual rights. Civil society organizations, on the other hand, may focus on broader social justice issues, pushing for policies that address systemic inequalities and promote inclusive security practices. Industry leaders contribute valuable insights into the operational and technological aspects of security, highlighting practical considerations and potential innovations. Meanwhile, government agencies provide the regulatory framework and enforcement mechanisms necessary to implement and oversee policy measures effectively.

To facilitate effective stakeholder engagement, it is necessary to employ strategies that encourage active participation and collaboration. Multi-stakeholder dialogues and workshops offer platforms for open discussion, allowing participants to share their views and cocreate solutions. These forums can break down silos, fostering understanding and cooperation across different sectors. Leveraging technology for virtual engagement platforms expands the reach of these discussions, enabling broader participation regardless of geographical constraints. This technological approach democratizes the policymaking process, ensuring that a wider array of voices is heard and considered. Such platforms can also facilitate ongoing communication, allowing stakeholders to remain engaged throughout the policy development and implementation phases.

Examples of successful stakeholder engagement initiatives illustrate the potential impact of collaborative policy development. In many local communities, collaborative efforts have led to policies that are more attuned to the specific needs and challenges of the area. These initiatives often involve partnerships between community organizations, local governments, and private security firms, resulting in tailored solutions that enhance public safety while respecting community values. Public-private partnerships in security strategy design further demonstrate the power of stakeholder engagement. By aligning the expertise and resources of both the public and private sectors, these partnerships can develop innovative and effective security strategies that address complex challenges. The success of these initiatives underscores the importance of involving diverse stakeholders in the policymaking process, as it leads to more robust and resilient security frameworks.

Involving stakeholders in security policy development is not just a procedural formality; it is a strategic imperative that enriches the process and outcomes. By embracing diverse perspectives, policymakers can craft solutions that are both innovative and grounded in the realities of those affected by security measures. This approach enables a sense of shared responsibility and commitment, ultimately leading to policies that better serve the public interest. As you consider the role of stakeholder engagement in your own work or studies, reflect on how these strategies and examples can inform your approach to policy development, ensuring that it is both inclusive and impactful.

The Role of Private Policing in a Changing Global Landscape

The landscape of private policing is shifting dramatically as global dynamics evolve. Geopolitical changes increasingly influence security priorities, compelling nations and businesses to adapt swiftly. Political instability, regional conflicts, and shifting alliances create a tapestry of security challenges that require innovative solutions. For instance, the rise of geopolitical tensions in certain regions has heightened the demand for private security services, as companies seek to protect their assets and personnel in volatile areas. In this context, private policing offers a flexible and responsive alternative to traditional state security apparatuses, capable of adapting quickly to new threats and uncertainties.

Economic trends further shape the demand for private security. As global economies fluctuate, the need for robust security measures becomes more pronounced. Economic growth in emerging markets often outpaces the development of public infrastructure, including law enforcement. This gap presents an opportunity for private security firms to step in, providing essential services where public resources are strained or insufficient. The growing interdependence of global markets also means that security concerns can no longer be confined to national borders. Companies engaged in international trade and investment rely on private security to face the complexities of operating in diverse regulatory environments, ensuring compliance and minimizing risk.

Confronting the intricacies of international regulations poses a significant challenge for private security firms. Each country has its own set of laws and standards, which can vary widely and often change. This complexity demands a high degree of flexibility and expertise from security providers, who must remain vigilant to ensure compliance and avoid legal pitfalls. Yet, these challenges also open doors for cross-border cooperation. Collaborative efforts between nations and security firms can lead to shared best practices and coordinated responses to transnational threats, such as terrorism and human trafficking. These partnerships are required in a world where crime and insecurity know no borders.

Private security has a pivotal role in addressing global challenges and contributing to international peacekeeping missions and cybersecurity initiatives. In peacekeeping, private firms often provide logistical support, personnel training, and on-the-ground security, complementing the efforts of international organizations. Their involvement increases the scope and efficiency of peacekeeping operations, enabling missions to achieve their objectives with greater effectiveness. Similarly, in the realm of cybersecurity, private security firms collaborate with governments and businesses to secure critical infrastructure and protect against cyber threats. By leveraging their expertise and resources, they bolster global efforts to safeguard digital spaces and maintain the integrity of information systems.

The impact of private security on international security is evident in various case studies. In humanitarian crises, private security firms have played a key role in ensuring the safety of aid workers and the secure distribution of resources. Their presence allows humanitarian organizations to operate in high-risk environments, delivering aid to those in need while minimizing the risks to personnel and assets. Cross-national security partnerships in counterterrorism demonstrate the power of collaboration between private and public entities. By sharing intelligence, resources, and expertise, these partnerships enhance the ability to detect and neutralize threats, contributing to global security efforts.

Throughout this chapter, we've explored how private policing is adapting to a complex global landscape. As geopolitical and economic forces continue to evolve, the role of private security will undoubtedly expand, offering innovative solutions to emerging challenges. The flexibility and expertise of private security firms make them indispensable partners in navigating these uncertain times. As the discussion shifts to the broader implications of these developments, consider how private policing can continue to contribute to a safer and more secure world.

Conclusion

Throughout this exploration of private policing, we have embarked on a journey through the annals of history, tracing the evolution of this vital aspect of modern law enforcement. From the watchmen of ancient times to the high-tech security firms of today, private policing has undergone a remarkable transformation. Yet, at its core, the mission remains the same: to ensure the safety and well-being of the communities it serves.

As we have seen, the growth of private security has been shaped by a myriad of factors from the industrial revolution to the post-9/11 era. Each milestone has brought new challenges and opportunities, pushing the industry to adapt and innovate. The rise of organized security firms in the 19th century laid the foundation for the professionalization of the field, while the technological advancements of recent decades have opened up new frontiers in crime prevention and risk management.

But with great power comes great responsibility. As private policing has grown in scope and influence, so too has the need for robust legal and ethical frameworks to guide its operations. The complex web of laws and regulations governing the industry can be daunting, but it is essential to ensure accountability and uphold the rights of all citizens. By adhering to the highest standards of professionalism and integrity, private security firms can build trust with the public and serve as vital partners in the broader law enforcement ecosystem.

Technology has been a game changer in this regard. From AI-powered surveillance systems to advanced cybersecurity protocols, the tools of the trade have never been more sophisticated. But as we have learned, technology is only as effective as the people who wield it. That is why continuous training and professional development are so crucial. By staying at the forefront of emerging trends and best practices, security professionals can harness the power of innovation to better serve their clients and communities.

Of course, no discussion of private policing would be complete without acknowledging the importance of collaboration. The most successful security strategies are those that leverage the strengths of both the public and private sectors. By working together, law enforcement agencies and security firms can pool their resources and expertise to create a more comprehensive and effective safety net. From joint training exercises to shared intelligence networks, the possibilities for cooperation are endless.

However, collaboration is not just about tactics and resources. It is also about building relationships and fostering trust. That is why community engagement is such a vital part of modern policing. By involving local stakeholders in the development of security policies and initiatives, private firms can ensure that their efforts are aligned with the needs and values of the communities they serve. This kind of grassroots approach not only enhances the effectiveness of security measures but also helps build a sense of shared responsibility for public safety.

As we look to the future of private policing, it is clear that the challenges will only continue to grow. From geopolitical instability to economic uncertainty, the global landscape is fraught with risks and uncertainties. But with challenge comes opportunity. By embracing innovation, collaboration, and community engagement, private security firms can play a vital role in shaping a safer and more secure world for all.

So, what can you do to be a part of this important work? Start by staying informed and engaged. Keep up with the latest developments in the field, and don't be afraid to ask questions and challenge assumptions. Advocate for policies and practices that prioritize transparency, accountability, and ethical conduct. And most importantly, never lose sight of the human element. Remember that behind every statistic and every headline, there are real people whose lives are impacted by the work of private security professionals.

As you embark on your own journey in this field, whether as a student, policymaker, or practitioner, I encourage you to keep the lessons of this book close at hand. The insights and strategies contained within these pages are not just abstract concepts but practical tools for navigating the complex world of private policing. By applying them in your own work and studies, you can make a meaningful difference in the lives of those around you.

So, let us go forth with a renewed sense of purpose and a steadfast commitment to the principles of justice, fairness, and public service. Together, we can build a future in which private policing is not just a necessary evil but a powerful force for good. A future in which every citizen can feel safe, secure, and protected, no matter who they are or where they live. That is the vision that drives this work, and it is a vision that I believe we can all get behind.

About the Authors

The journey of Professors Lisa Stolzenberg and Stewart D'Alessio in the dynamic field of criminology resembles the chapters of a compelling crime novel. Individually, they are formidable scholars; together, they have redefined the boundaries of criminological research. Their collaborative journey highlights the confluence of their passions and demonstrates the power of synergy in academic pursuits.

Upon completing their undergraduate studies, Stolzenberg and D'Alessio met in 1986 at Florida State University while pursuing postgraduate degrees in criminology. A casual conversation over pizza evolved into a brainstorming session and a collaborative partnership that has lasted nearly four decades. After initially accepting faculty positions at Indiana-Purdue University Fort Wayne, they relocated to Florida International University (FIU) in Miami, where they spent their childhood years. Today, they are tenured professors of criminology at FIU's Steven J. Green School of International and Public Affairs.

The combined expertise of Drs. Stolzenberg and D'Alessio and their passion for criminology have led to significant contributions in the fields of criminology and criminal justice. Working in tandem, they have published numerous books and influential scholarly articles on topics such as race and crime, criminal sentencing, and criminal justice policy. They were also instrumental in developing two unique degree programs in the United States: the PhD in International Crime and Justice and the Bachelor of Science in Crime Science.

Today, criminologists worldwide are inspired by their dedication, innovative spirit, and ability to break down silos in the pursuit of knowledge. Their story is a testament to the power of collaboration and the profound impact that committed individuals can have when they unite to pursue knowledge and justice.

References

Abrahamsen, R. (2012, July 17). *The Olympics, and the rise and dangers of private security*. Centre for International Policy Studies. https://www.cips-cepi.ca/2012/07/17/the-olympics-and-the-rise-and-dangers-of-private-security/

Andrews, L. (2023). *Private security: Trends and innovations*. AGS. https://www.agsprotect.com/blog/private-security-trends-and-innovations

Anon. (n.d.). *Codes of ethics for private security management and private security employees*. NCJRS. https://www.ojp.gov/ncjrs/virtual-library/abstracts/codes-ethics-private-security-management-and-private-security

Artificial intelligence in predictive policing issue brief. (n.d.). NAACP. https://naacp.org/resources/artificial-intelligence-predictive-policing-issue-brief

Biometrics and privacy – issues and challenges. (n.d.). Office of the Victorian Information Commissioner. https://ovic.vic.gov.au/privacy/resources-for-organisations/biometrics-and-privacy-issues-and-challenges/

Blair-Frasier, R. (2024). *Mentorship key in building security careers*. *Security Magazine*. https://www.securitymagazine.com/articles/100578-mentorship-key-in-building-security-careers

Bosman, S. (2023). *Public-private partnerships in crime prevention: Challenges and recommendations*. European Crime Prevention Network. https://eucpn.org/sites/default/files/document/files/2308_ENG_PAPER_Private%20partnerships_LR_0.pdf

Bowles, M. (2022). *The evolution of private security*. Top Guard Security. https://topguardinc.com/the-evolution-of-private-security/

Certified Protection Professional (CPP). (n.d.). ASIS. https://www.asisonline.org/certification/certified-protection-professional-cpp/

Community-based approaches to enhance public safety. (n.d.). Guards on Call. https://guardsoncall.us/community-based-approaches-to-enhance-public-safety/

Conley, T., Wasylyshyn, M., & Tobin, T. (2024). *Public-private partnerships: A keystone for safer communities worldwide*. ASIS. https://www.asisonline.org/publications--resources/news/blog/2024/public-private-partnerships-a-keystone-for-safer-communities-worldwide/

Contributor CSM. (2025). *SWOT analysis: Private security companies. City Security*. https://citysecuritymagazine.com/risk-management/swot-analysis-private-security-companies/

Crisis communications for law enforcement agencies. (n.d.). Blackberry. https://www.blackberry.com/us/en/solutions/critical-event-management/crisis-communications-law-enforcement

Cyber attacks on security firms: What we've learned from case studies. (2024). El Dorado Insurance. https://www.eldoradoinsurance.com/security-industry-news/the-rising-threat-of-cyber-attacks-on-security-firms-lessons-learned-from-case-studies/

Encyclopædia Britannica. (2025). *Pinkerton National Detective Agency*. In *Encyclopædia Britannica*. https://www.britannica.com/topic/Pinkerton-National-Detective-Agency

Examining the U.S. Capitol attack. (n.d.). United States Senate. https://www.hsgac.senate.gov/wp-content/uploads/imo/media/doc/HSGAC&RulesFullReport_ExaminingU.S.CapitolAttack.pdf

50-state security licensing compliance guide. (n.d.). Harbor Compliance. https://www.harborcompliance.com/security-license

Gonzalez, M. (2023). *The impact of the fourth industrial revolution on physical security. Security 101.* https://www.security101.com/blog/the-impact-of-the-fourth-industrial-revolution-on-physical-security

Goosman, A. (2025). *Public vs. private sector emergency & crisis management: Diverging missions, common fundamentals.* LinkedIn. https://www.linkedin.com/pulse/public-vs-private-sector-emergency-crisis-management-ashley-xg70e

Kitteringham, G. (2020, July). *Guard training programs: A development guide.* ASIS. https://www.asisonline.org/security-management-magazine/articles/2020/07/guard-training-programs-a-development-guide/

Kohl, G. (2018, June 1). *GDPR and the security industry.* SIA. https://www.securityindustry.org/2018/06/01/gdpr-and-the-security-industry/

LeClair, J., Abraham, S., & Shih, L. (2013). An interdisciplinary approach to educating an effective cyber security workforce. In *Proceedings of the 2013 ACM conference on Innovation and technology in computer science education* (pp. 71–78). ACM. https://dl.acm.org/doi/10.1145/2528908.2528923

Pastore, T. J. (2025). *Legal brief: Drone regulation in the spotlight. Security Info Watch.* https://www.securityinfowatch.com/perimeter-security/robotics/unmanned-aerial-vehicles-drones/article/55250586/legal-brief-drone-regulation-in-the-spotlight

Private Security Industry Act 2001. (2001). legislation.gov.uk. https://www.legislation.gov.uk/ukpga/2001/12/contents

Richardson, R., Schultz, J. M., & Crawford, K. (2019). Dirty data, bad predictions: How civil rights violations impact police data, predictive policing systems, and justice. *New York University Law Review Online, 94*(15). https://www.nyulawreview.org/wp-content/uploads/2019/04/NYULawReview-94-Richardson_etal-FIN.pdf

Stephens, D., Stephens, B., & Pesta, G. (n.d.). *Forging problem-solving partnerships to address unprecedented community safety challenges: Police and private security relationships*. Florida State University Policing, Security Technology, and Private Security Research & Policy Institute. https://criminology.fsu.edu/sites/g/files/upcbnu3076/files/1%20Cent er%202024/Police%20%26%20Private%20Security%20Roundtable %20Final%20Report.pdf

Somerville, P. (2024). *The power of collaboration: The importance of intelligence sharing in cyber defense*. Pulsar Security. https://blog.pulsarsecurity.com/the-power-of-collaboration-the-importance-of-intelligence-sharing

TAK technology takes center stage. (n.d.). Synergy. https://www.synergybis.com/2025/02/24/how-uscg-itak-secured-super-bowl-lix-in-new-orleans/

Three ways AI is a game-changer for security operations center. (n.d.). KPMG. https://kpmg.com/us/en/articles/2024/three-ways-ai-game-changer-security-operations-center.html

Wade v. Byles, 83 F.3d 902 (7th Cir. 1996).

Wildhorn, S. (1975). *Issues in private security*. Rand. https://www.rand.org/pubs/papers/P5422.html

www.ingramcontent.com/pod-product-compliance
Lightning Source LLC
Chambersburg PA
CBHW072200270326
41930CB00011B/2498